Heinrich Böll

Die verlorene Ehre der Katharina Blum

Donal McLaughlin

Lecturer in German,
Heriot-Watt University.

UNIVERSITY OF GLASGOW
FRENCH AND GERMAN PUBLICATIONS
1992

University of Glasgow French and German Publications

Series Editors: Mark G. Ward (German)
Geoff Woollen (French)

Consultant Editors : Colin Smethurst
Kenneth Varty

Modern Languages Building, University of Glasgow,
Glasgow G12 8QL, Scotland.

First published 1988; reprinted 1992, 1995

Printed by Castle Cary Press, Somerset BA20 2HP

ISBN 0 85261 257 5

CONTENTS

ABBREVIATIONS

To reduce the number of footnotes, the following abbreviations are used in the text. Only a brief indication of each source is given here, full details can be found in the bibliography.

Abbr.   Source

E2   Böll, *Essayistische Schriften und Reden 2*, Cologne 1978

K   *Die verlorene Ehre der Katharina Blum*, dtv and Harrap editions

KT   *The Lost Honour of Katharina Blum*, Penguin translation

SECONDARY LITERATURE

BM   Bach/Meinhof, 'Introduction' to Harrap edition of *Katharina Blum*

CL   Christian Linder (book), Cologne 1975

KB   Keith Bullivant (article), *GLL*, 1986

MD   Manfred Durzak (interview), in: Böll, *Interviews I*, Cologne 1978, 321-347

MR   Mark W. Rectanus, (article), *GQ*, 1986

OD   [Inter Nationes] (book), Bonn 1985

PP   Philip Payne (article), *NGS*, 1978

RK   Richard Kilborn (book), Glasgow 1984

RW   Rhys Williams (article), *CQ*, 1979

Chapter One

Writer and Background

The Writer Heinrich Böll

The immediate public response to the death of Heinrich Böll (21 December 1917—16 July 1985) illustrates particularly well the unique position held by this author in post-war German literature, and indeed society. Flags were flown at half mast, television schedules rearranged to accommodate tributes and film versions of the writer's works. Queues formed outside bookshops on the morning after his death. Large quantities of his books sold. An initiative was launched to have a 'Heinrich-Böll-Platz' in his home city of Cologne; seven schools were soon to be named after him.[1] No less a personage than the President of the Federal Republic of Germany, Richard von Weizsäcker, paid tribute to the author: 'With Heinrich Böll one of the great men of German literature has gone from us. He stood for freedom of the mind wherever it was endangered. He was uncomfortable and pugnacious, he caused offence and generated respect. We shall miss his courageous, committed, aware and constantly warning voice' (OD 57). Michael Butler has rightly commented in this regard: 'It is hard to imagine any other European writer whose death would provoke similar sentiments, or indeed much comment at all, from a Head of State'.[2] In fact, von Weizsäcker even attended Böll's funeral; he planned to visit, in addition, a later memorial service in Cologne organised by Böll's fellow writers - until the press baron Axel Springer died on 22 September 1985 and another funeral beckoned. The great irony of the President's 'Termindilemma' will become apparent when we consider Böll's previous clashes with the Springer consortium.[3]

A large number of obituaries sought to do justice to the achievements of Heinrich Böll. Again and again, reporters pointed to Böll 's role—imposed on the reluctant author by his German and international public —as the conscience of the nation, 'a moral authority' (OD 55), 'perhaps the last saint of literature' (OD 62). The personal qualities of the man did not escape the obituarists: his charisma, his humility, his integrity, his credibility. The former President of the Federal Republic and Chairman of the Social Democrats (SPD), Willy Brandt, asserted: 'In his books as in public life Heinrich Böll was the voice of decency: incorruptible, uncompromising and when necessary sharp and honest. The subject of his literary creation and his political commitment was the dignity of man' (OD 57). Tellingly, the concerns of this 'tireless defender of human rights' (OD 55) extended beyond the borders of his native Germany—to Central America, the Warsaw Pact countries and the Third World. Heinrich Vormweg argued in this respect: 'all the weak, the distressed, the oppressed and persecuted have lost an irreplaceable advocate in Heinrich Böll' (OD 14); Marcel Reich-Ranicki stressed: 'countless people all over the world owe him so much; many owe him their lives' (OD 11). These facets of the author's achievement more than justify Reich-Ranicki 's judgement that Böll represented 'more than a writer' (OD 7).

Naturally, the obituaries also lauded Böll's literary accomplishments; but, more than that, the critics posited that the name of Böll was effectively synonymous with the notion of post-1945 German writing. The *Frankfurter Neue Presse* affirmed: 'Without forgetting or diminishing the merit of others, the concept of a new German post-war literature is linked for a large public with the name of Heinrich Böll. In this context only Günter Grass approaches him' (OD 58). It is indisputable that after the separatism and censorship of the Third Reich (1933-1945) Böll assisted the Germans to re-establish points of contact with world literature. Keith Bullivant, in a paper given at the Institute of Germanic Studies in London in 1985 to commemorate the writer, observed:

> World sales of his work exceeded 31 million copies before his death, over 12 million of these in the Federal Republic; in terms of world readership, therefore, Böll whose work has been translated into 45 languages, succeeded in reaching far more people than any other German writer before him, while, in the peculiar context of the post-war period, he managed to bridge the gulf between East and West better than any other author of his time. (KB 245)

Bullivant does not hesitate to emphasise the magnitude of Böll's importance: 'No writer from anywhere else in the world can, in the post-war period, lay claim to this body of achievement and recognition' (KB 245). Given these proportions, Walter Höllerer's appraisal seems in no way exaggerated: 'Für mich ist der Tod von Heinrich Böll ein Bruch im Continuum der deutschsprachigen Literatur nach 1945'.[4]

Which qualities of Böll's literary *œuvre* justify such massive claims? The historical background to his works forms one especially valuable aspect. Böll, born in 1917, grew up in the Weimar Republic and experienced the seizure of power by the Nazis in 1933 as a sixteen-year-old (precisely the age at which many young British students first encounter his books nowadays). The period of the Third Reich thus coincides with twelve formative years in the author's life: Böll is twenty-eight when the war ends in 1945. Naturally, he presents and probes the Nazi era in his *œuvre*. As such, his writings explore not only a major incision in the history of Germany and Europe in the twentieth century; the holocaust represents, over and above that, perhaps the worst atrocity ever perpetrated by humankind. Böll, in his invaluable literary investigation of this man-made tragedy, aims to combat the propensity of nations and individuals for amnesia about the (Nazi) past, and thus to help prevent any repetition of such inhumanity.

At the same time, Böll's publications, all of which appeared after 1945, reflect the history of the Federal Republic of Germany (founded in 1949) as does, arguably, the work of none of his contemporaries. We find the various phases mirrored in his *œuvre:* 'the 'Heimkehrer' ('returning soldiers' or 'homecomers'), the hand-to-mouth existence in the ruins, the 'Währungsreform' ('currency reform', 1948), the gradual establishment of prosperity (1950s and 1960s), the re-formation of the Army (1954/5), the burden of the Nazi past, the time of anarchic protest (1968) and of the terrorist threat (1970s) ' (KB 246). Whereas major works by his writer colleagues Günter Grass (born 1927) and Siegfried Lenz (born 1926) focus on Danzig and Masuria respectively, i.e. territories now part of Poland, Böll's fiction is firmly anchored in the Rhineland of his times. Such treatment of the here and now, this focus on topical themes and problems, make the writer, as Keith Bullivant argues, almost unique beyond the boundaries of Germany too: 'it is difficult, if not impossible, to think of another author whose work so encapsulates the social, cultural and political history of a state from its inception up to the point of his death' (KB 245). Clearly, critics were not reluctant to attribute enormous importance to the author.

The fact that his settings, characters and themes prove so familiar no doubt contributed to the great popularity and impact of Heinrich

Böll, a writer renowned for being accessible, readable and translatable, and for his striking satirical humour. Not long after the author was awarded the Nobel Prize for Literature in 1972, a reviewer in the *Times Literary Supplement* made, in this respect, a telling comparison with the previous German recipients Thomas Mann (1875-1955) and Hermann Hesse (1877-1962): 'Böll's fictional world is far removed from the often exclusive and rarified spheres in which Mann's and Hesse's characters move. Böll is concerned with an immediately recognizable world of definable relationships through which we can elucidate time past and time present. He creates individual profiles, for whom he expresses a deep compassion and strong sense of identification'.[5] The last words of this assessment hint at the uncompromising moral decency and strong commitment so characteristic of Böll. The author battled against the repression of the past by German society, opposed the uncaring forces of capitalism and commercialisation, and protested against the intrusion of the State in the lives of ordinary individuals. Böll defended human rights vigorously. He emphasised the emotional needs of human beings too and stressed the need for charity in everyday life. The depth of the convictions of this often controversial writer impressed, ultimately, readers and critics alike.

Böll 's literary stature is founded on an *œuvre* which spans four decades. To the knowledge of critics, he first published after 1945 when his short stories appeared in periodicals. Well-known literary depictions of the horrors of war and the post-war ruins by Böll and Wolfgang Borchert (1921-1947) have attracted the labels 'Kriegsgeschichten' and 'Trümmerliteratur'. Böll's first book publication, *Der Zug war pünktlich* (1949), concentrated on the war too. Subsequent novels switched attention to the later post-war years. *Und sagte kein einziges Wort* (1953), a study of the marital crisis of Fred and Käte Bogner, reflects the material poverty and the loss of spiritual faith characteristic of the Germany of the time; *Das Brot der frühen Jahre* (1955) shows how following a chance encounter with a young woman, the hero opts out of the Germany of the Restoration and yearns for the abandoned values and unfulfilled hopes and aspirations of the 'early years '. Two other—larger—novels from the 1950s, *Haus ohne Hüter* (1954) and *Billard um halb zehn* (1959), illustrate how the Nazi past continues to play a role in the narrative present. Böll's *Irisches Tagebuch* (1957), a record, now entertaining, now moving, of his response to Ireland during numerous visits, should be of special interest for British readers.

Throughout the 1950s, Böll continued to publish, in addition, short stories—and satires such as *Doktor Murkes gesammeltes Schweigen* (1958) which proved especially popular with the reading public; *Ende einer Dienstfahrt* (1966) and *Berichte zur Gesinnungslage der Nation* (1975) might be viewed as extended versions of this genre. In the 1960s, as throughout his literary career, Böll wrote poems, radio plays and essays besides. In 1963, *Ansichten eines Clowns,* his most accomplished novel so far, took critical stock of developments in West German society under the chancellorship of Konrad Adenauer (1949-1963). These various publications all precede the period of his life which includes the composition of *Die verlorene Ehre der Katharina Blum.*

In the last fifteen years of his life, the author completed four major prose works. In 1971, a novel, reckoned by many to be Böll's best, appeared. Just as *Billard um halb zehn,* set in 1958, sought twelve years earlier to present a 'historische Summe'[6] by means of its focus on three generations of the Fähmel family, so *Gruppenbild mit Dame,* with its depiction of the heroine Leni, attempted a summation of the years 1922-1970. *Die verlorene Ehre der Katharina Blum* (1974) mirrored the anxious response of West German society to the terrorist threat posed by the notorious Baader-Meinhof group in the early 1970s. Five years later, *Fürsorgliche Belagerung* (1979), which depicts how security cameras installed for the protection of the Tolm family come to dominate their lives, points up 'the uneasy political atmosphere of suspicion and insecurity in West Germany at the end of the 1970s, resulting from urban terrorism and the government's attempts to combat it'.[7] A fourth work, *Frauen vor Flußlandschaft* (1985), completed not long before Böll's death and published shortly afterwards, tackles the Federal Republic of the 1980s; Böll sets this novel in the West German capital Bonn, home of the 'Bundestag', the legislative assembly of the country. The formal innovations of these four works represent the result of Böll's increasingly ambitious endeavours, from the 1950s onwards, to experiment with narrative techniques.

This brief, by no means exhaustive summary of Böll 's writings yields some impression of the dimensions of his *œuvre.* From it, we can discern too the place occupied by *Die verlorene Ehre der Katharina Blum* in this impressive body of work.

Historical Background 1967-1977

At the beginning of the 1970s, the Baader-Meinhof terrorist group, by means of its violent 'assault on West German consensus politics', posed probably 'the most serious domestic threat to the political legitimacy of the Federal Republic since its foundation in 1949'.[8] This period thus marks a key 'historical conjuncture in an emergent state' (RK 2). Accordingly, Böll's 'Erzählung', an examination of 'how violence develops and where it can lead' (KT 3) first published in 1974, represents an example of 'the literary text as a response to a sociohistorical context' (MR 253) and must be studied as such. It is therefore necessary at this point to present in some detail the major incidents of those times.

Violence had flared in the Federal Republic in the late 1960s with the advent of the student movement.[9] In June 1967, demonstrations against a visit by the Shah of Iran took place in West Berlin; a policeman shot dead the student Benno Ohnesorg. In April 1968, the student leader Rudi Dutschke survived an assassination attempt but suffered serious injury. Easter 1968 saw demonstrations throughout the country against the Springer Verlag and its *BILD-Zeitung* (which later served as a model for the ZEITUNG in *Die verlorene Ehre der Katharina Blum*). Commentators have observed in this respect: '*Bild* had right from the beginning of the student movement taken an unabashed strong anti-student line. With headlines forever suggesting links between students, Communists and violence, *Bild* antagonized and whipped up emotions about what was never—not even at the height of the action in 1968— more than a modest student movement' (BM xix). In fact, the levels of extraparliamentary opposition (APO) troubled the governing authorities so much that 'Notstandsgesetze' were passed. These emergency laws granted a committee special powers at times of national crisis. Such legislation reflects the at that time growing obsession on the part of the general public and the German press with the issue of 'Gewalt'.

Terrorist activity in the Federal Republic in the early 1970s tested West German political leaders to a degree disproportionate to the actual size of the Baader-Meinhof group and to the extent of the support it commanded. Public concern about violence became yet more accentuated as a result. Critics have identified 'the amazing overreaction ', manipulated by the press,—'a turbulence, hardly rational, springing from profound anxieties, suspicions, fears, not explicable in terms of the actual incidents' (BM xxii). Not that events were not dramatic. On 14 April 1970, Ulrike Meinhof assisted in the escape of Andreas Baader who had been imprisoned for his involvement in arson attacks on shopping stores in Frankfurt in April 1968. In the summer of 1970, the so-called 'erste Generation'—including Horst Mahler and Ulrike Meinhof—were being trained in the camps of the Palestinian terrorist organisation Al Fatah in Jordan. September 1970 saw their first bank robberies in West Berlin. Throughout 1970 and 1971, passports were stolen, banks robbed; the name 'Rote Armee Faktion' (RAF) was coined. On 15 July 1971, police shot Petra Schelm, a member of the group, in Hamburg, where three months later the RAF killed the policeman Norbert Schmidt. In May 1972, the group inflicted several bomb attacks on American institutions in Germany, on police stations, and on the Springer Verlag. In June, in rapid succession, Andreas Baader, Holger Meins, Jan Carl Raspe, Gudrun Ensslin and Ulrike Meinhof were arrested.

The Baader-Meinhof group had been active for merely two years before their arrest; their crimes seem mild when compared with the melodramatic terrorist activities of the 'second generation' later. Nevertheless, their actions gave rise to a witch-hunt mentality and near-hysteria in West Germany such that the 'criminalisation of protest' (RK 9) resulted. Given this volatile political climate, the atmosphere of aggression and violence, the feelings of insecurity and vulnerability, it is not surprising that Böll aroused so much controversy with the publication of his article 'Will Ulrike Meinhof Gnade oder freies Geleit?' in *Der Spiegel* of 10 January 1972. Böll was kicking against the pricks. He published and was damned. There followed a smear campaign against the author which has parallels in the character assassination suffered by Katharina Blum in his later 'Erzählung'.

Böll's article attracted the angry charge that he played down the dangers posed by the Baader-Meinhof group. The author countered: 'Ich habe versucht, die Proportionen zurechtzurücken' (E2 555). Despite emphatically rejecting the means and ends of the group, Böll was nonetheless accused of sympathising with the terrorists. The author himself later criticised weaknesses in the article: for him, it failed to depict the escalation in violence in the Federal Republic; it failed too to break new ground in the public debate since the other parties managed to adhere stubbornly to old positions. To the criticism that his essay may have contravened certain standards and rules, however, Böll replied: 'Man muß zu weit gehen' (E2 554). This attitude recalls the stance taken by the Mexican writer Carlos Fuentes: 'if writers don 't say it, then it won 't be said'.[10] Writers have a duty to ensure that certain ideas enter and remain in the public consciousness, even if they offend the prevailing ideology. Tellingly, variations on the remark 'Fragen dürfen wird man doch wohl' (E2 545) recur thrice in Böll's article, as he seeks confirmation, not without irony, that the individual remains morally and legally entitled to pose critical and pertinent questions. The questions raised by Böll in his article may not necessarily satisfy specialists in the field of politics and media studies, but they are valid probings nonetheless.

The main weakness of the article may in fact lie in the title. Its sole focus on one controversial figure, which could be misinterpreted as an unqualified plea for mercy for Meinhof, does the wider focus of the actual article an injustice. In another context, Böll has defined its subject-matter more successfully as 'das öffentliche Bewußtsein in Sachen Ulrike Meinhof' (E2 551). As an appraisal of the public's perception of, and reaction to, matters involving Meinhof, Böll's article seems a fair and worthwhile exercise. He attacks the *BILD-Zeitung,* the only source of information for many readers, highlighting indisputable inaccuracies, distortions and politically slanted headlines in the coverage of the Baader-Meinhof activities. He asserts: 'Das ist nicht mehr kryptofaschistisch, nicht mehr faschistoid, das ist nackter Faschismus. Verhetzung, Lüge, Dreck' (E2 545). Böll contrasts *BILD* reports with a police statement which is 'nüchtern, sachlich, angesichts der Indizien plausibel, legitim' (E2 542). The author who considers that the newspaper headlines incite readers to violence, encourages the public, the police, judges and journalists to read instead the publications of the Baader-Meinhof group in order to be better informed about their goals and motivation. In this way, Böll tackles the problem of disinformation and its deleterious effect on public opinion.

Without minimizing the threat posed by terrorists—'Ich wiederhole: Kein Zweifel—Ulrike Meinhof lebt im Kriegszustand mit dieser Gesellschaft' (E2 546)—, Böll insists, moreover, that society must monitor carefully its response to that peril, and guard against the emergence of 'totale Gnadenlosigkeit' (E2 547). The author invites those in power to recall the discrimination and persecution typical of the Third Reich, and to ensure that no institutionalised witch-hunt is launched against any minority in the Federal Republic. In January 1972, five months before the arrest of the leading group members, Böll anticipates their violent deaths (in 1976 and 1977) and protests that this fate should not be regarded as inevitable:

> Muß es so kommen? Will Ulrike Meinhof, daß es so kommt? Will sie Gnade oder wenigstens freies Geleit? Selbst wenn sie keines von beiden will, einer muß es ihr anbieten. Dieser Prozeß muß stattfinden, er muß der lebenden Ulrike Meinhof gemacht werden, in Gegenwart der Weltöffentlichkeit. Sonst ist nicht nur sie und der Rest ihrer Gruppe verloren, es wird weiter stinken in der deutschen Publizistik, es wird weiter stinken in der deutschen Rechtgeschichte. (E2 548)

Böll does not request a free pardon for Meinhof. He places an onus on society to ensure that, for its part, it responds fairly, justly, reasonably. Society must avoid a biased, brute response; the press and the legal system must acquit themselves well or risk condemning themselves. Böll argued for safe conduct ('freies Geleit') and a public trial for Meinhof; and for Axel Springer to be tried too 'wegen Volks-verhetzung'(E2 548). Tragically, West German society did not heed Böll 's reasoned warnings. Further deathly violence and hysteria ensued.

Die verlorene Ehre der Katharina Blum , with its spotlight—as the subtitle indicates—firmly on the theme of violence, appeared in 1974; the film version of the book was first screened in 1975. We must bear in mind not only that these works were created in the violent historical context outlined above; but also that subsequent events further heightened the fear of violence of the West German public, and thus no doubt jaundiced its initial response to both the book and film. In April 1975, an RAF commando attacked the German Embassy in Stockholm. On 21 May, the trial of the 'hard core' of the Baader-Meinhof group commenced in Stuttgart-Stammheim. On 9 May 1976, Ulrike Meinhof was found dead in her cell. In August 1977, the RAF murdered the prominent lawyer ('Generalbundesanwalt') Buback. On 5 September, the leading industrialist Hanns Martin Schleyer was kidnapped. On 13 October, a Lufthansa Boeing 747 was hijacked; it was stormed by a special unit, the GSG 9, in Mogadischu on 18 October. Within hours, Baader, Raspe and Ennslin were found dead in their cells in Stammheim. Execution or suicide? That was the question. Schleyer was murdered in retaliation on 20 October. The burial of the terrorists in a city cemetery met with strong resistance. These events of autumn 1977 have been documented in an important collective film, *Deutschland*

im Herbst (1977/1978), directed by Alexander Kluge, Edgar Reitz,
Volker Schlöndorff and Rainer Werner Fassbinder, among others.
Böll contributed to the script.

Without wishing in any way to underestimate or minimize recent
political unrest in the United Kingdom, we should recognise that
post-war generations of readers in Britain probably cannot conceive
of the nation-wide hysteria sparked by the events of the decade 1967-
1977 in West Germany. British citizens cannot relate such reactions
to personal experience. The scenario may appear familiar to the
population of Northern Ireland, but the British 'Biedermann' has
seldom been unsettled by bomb-carrying 'Brandstifter' ('fire-
raisers') attacking mainland Britain. Similarly, the strategic defence
initiative which was the Falklands War took place at the other end of
the earth while waves of jingoism and nationalism succoured the
nation. The inner city riots of the 1980s in Brixton and Toxteth were
likewise too sporadic, scattered and short-lived to undermine the
sense of security of the British people as a whole. Moreover, such
instances of violence were not brought into even sharper relief by
memories of a not so distant Third Reich within our borders. It is
necessary to stress the differing experiences of British and German
citizens in this way because no reader can adequately assess Böll's
Die verlorene Ehre der Katharina Blum without a proper
appreciation of the catalogue of incidents in the Federal Republic
which culminated in the cataclysmic events of 1977.

Die verlorene Ehre der Katharina Blum brings together Böll the
story-teller, the writer of literary fiction, on the one hand, and Böll
the moralist, the publicist, the politically aware citizen ready to take
direct action, on the other. This combination attracted much
attention. Public awareness of the controversy surrounding his
article in 1972, and of his clashes with the Springer press, heightened
interest in the 'Erzählung'—the first piece of *belles lettres* ever to be
serialised in *Der Spiegel* . A first edition of 100,000 copies appeared
in August 1974; by the end of the year 200,000 had been sold; the
text was translated into eighteen languages; Springer discontinued the
publication of a 'Best-Seller-List' while the book remained popular.[11]
The film version, co-directed in 1975 by Volker Schlöndorff and
Margaretha von Trotta, made an immediate impression too: 'the first
production to be made under the terms of the new West German
film-television agreement of 1974' (RK 8), it represents, in terms of
box-office takings, one of the major successes of the New German
Cinema; such was the commercial success of the film in cinemas that

the television airing had twice to be postponed. The film, a major landmark in the careers of both Schlöndorff and von Trotta, demonstrated too the viability of left-wing cinema in West Germany. Important works such as Reinhard Hauff's *Messer im Kopf* (1978) and *Der Mann auf der Mauer* (1982), and von Trotta 's *Die bleierne Zeit* (1981) and *Rosa Luxemburg* (1985), soon followed. Von Trotta was also responsible for a dramatized version of the 'Erzählung' first staged in Bonn in 1976 and later performed in Castrop, Lucerne and Hamburg. [12] In 1984, ten years after the original publication, a television film adaptation, starring Mario Thomas and Kris Kristofferson, and entitled *The Lost Honor of Kathryn Beck*, was broadcast on CBS in the United States (MR 252); this re-make portrayed 'the violation of witnesses' rights and their victimization by the police and the media' in America (MR 263). A new opera, composed by Tilo Medek and planned for production in Gelsenkirchen in 1988, [13] further underlines the enduring relevance and topicality of Böll's text. Such continued and continuous interest shows *Die verlorene Ehre der Katharina Blum* to be an important work by a major literary figure.

Chapter Two

Aspects of

Die verlorene Ehre der Katharina Blum

Introduction

Die verlorene Ehre der Katharina Blum concentrates primarily on incidents which occur during a period of just five days in 1974. Despite the sensational nature of the events, no attempt is made to create, 'sustain or heighten any form of suspense for the reader. Instead, the third of the book's fifty-eight short sections draws attention to the key incidents. On 20 February, Katharina Blum meets and invites home Ludwig Götten who, unknown to her, initially, is a suspected terrorist under police observation. Between the unsuccessful attempt by the police the following morning to arrest Ludwig at her home and her murder of the journalist Tötges on 24 February, the police interrogate and the gutter press hounds Katharina Blum. Her experiences during this period, presented for the reader by an internal narrator, raise important issues which are given even greater emphasis by virtue of the fact that the element of suspense is played down. Before we can explore these themes, however, we must first discuss the rather complicated form of *Die verlorene Ehre der Katharina Blum*, for the presentation of the material affects again and again the ability of the reader or critic to make with any certainty statements regarding the case of Katharina Blum.

Form

The first page of *Die verlorene Ehre der Katharina Blum* records not only the title and subtitle of the text, but also the genre chosen by its author Heinrich Böll: 'Erzählung' (K 3). In the first sentence of its first section, however, the internal narrator describes the text alternatively as a 'Bericht' (K 7). This difference in terminology underlines how the text works on two levels. The unnamed narrator composes his 'Bericht' at a specific point in time, as a reaction to a specific situation, with, presumably, a specific purpose in mind; as such, the value of the resulting document is ephemeral. The author Heinrich Böll also writes from within a specific historical context, in response to specific experiences, and no doubt with specific aims, but Böll operates on another, higher plane: his selection of the literary genre 'Erzählung' points to his intention to create an imaginative and artistic work, more universal in purport, and with a value which transcends time. The existence of these two distinct levels has inspired Ruth Bach and Ulrike Hanna Meinhof to highlight a 'double focus' (BM xxxiii) in the text.

The 'Bericht'

In *Die verlorene Ehre der Katharina Blum,* Böll introduces an anonymous internal narrator who gathers, as indicated in the first section of his report, material on Katharina's case from three main, and several other secondary sources. Unlike 'der Verf.[asser]' in Böll's previous novel, *Gruppenbild mit Dame,* this narrator is never described and plays no part in the central events. He refers frequently to the difficulty he experiences, given the multiplicity of his sources, when trying to compile an accurate account of those events which took place between 20 and 24 February 1974. In a much-quoted statement from the second section, he provides the central metaphor of 'playing with puddles' to convey the notion of piecing together various fragments. References to this key passage recur repeatedly throughout the fifty-eight sections of the 'Bericht' when 'Stockungen, Stauungen, Versandungen, mißglückte Konduktionen und Quellen, die >zusammen nicht kommen können<, außerdem unterirdische Strömungen usw. usw.' (K 8) are highlighted. On the one hand, such references underline the constructed nature of the text, the aspect of 'Komposition' (K 8); on the other, given that they function as a leitmotif, the references lend greater coherence to what would otherwise have been a loose collection of fragmentary documents and statements. Too much significance should not, however, be read into this central metaphor. Böll has conceded elsewhere: 'Diese Zwischen-bemerkungen [...] formalistischer oder formaler Art sind eigentlich nur

Erholungspausen für den Autor' (MD 346).
The actual form of the narrator's report is at no point defined in exact terms. Which precise purpose does the internal narrator perceive for his 'Bericht'? The blurb of the Penguin translation *The Lost Honour of Katharina Blum* suggests that 'the formal, but not unsympathetic, manner of a police report' characterises the text. Rhys Williams, on the other hand, has argued: 'Böll's narrator adopts the persona of a newspaper correspondent. His investigation [...] is intended to serve as a model of responsible journalism' (RW 55). Manfred Durzak defines the text as a 'Gegen-Bericht zu den manipulierten und verfälschenden Zeitungsberichten' (MD 323). The neutral notion of 'Gegen-Bericht' is helpful, but some questions remain unanswered. What kind of readership does the narrator envisage for his report? Are the linguistic registers and stylistic devices employed in the text all appropriate to its selected form? Certainly, one may feel that the inclusion of complex considerations concerning the composition of the text might in fact stand in contradiction with its—ultimately undefined—original intentions. On this very point, Durzak has drawn the admission of a probable error from the author. Böll has conceded: 'Das ist wahrscheinlich falsch gewesen. Ich hätte das Ganze möglicherweise noch gröber halten sollen' (MD 345).

An undoubted strength of the form of the 'Bericht', on the other hand, lies in its ability to reflect the unattainability and indefinability of truth. Despite the multifarious sources available to the internal narrator, the truth, the whole truth, and nothing but the truth concerning Katharina Blum cannot be portrayed. Not even the narrator enjoys free access to all the information the reader might require. Böll's narrator, unlike the omniscient story-teller in more conventional prose works, is handicapped by the limitations of his restricted perspective. Since the internal narrator is not all-knowing, only incomplete evidence can be imparted to the reader. Consequently, the resulting text must be more open-ended than traditional narratives. This openness, this absence of ready-made, rounded conclusions, in turn challenges the reader to reconstruct as far as possible the sequence of events involving Katharina, and to arrive at an assessment of the situation based both on the available evidence and personal judgement. The reader soon establishes that in this modern literary text, as in everyday life, truth and external reality prove to be sufficiently complex in nature as to defy a full objective appraisal by any individual. The fragmentary quality of the text reflects in this way the inevitable limitations of human perception of reality. The complexity and rich ambiguities of the 'Bericht' counter, moreover, the dangerously simplistic 'facts' offered about Katharina Blum in the ZEITUNG.

We should realise too, however, that the narrator's personality can interfere with his presentation of the events of February 1974. The reader, wholly dependent on the narrator for an informed and fair account, cannot necessarily count with any confidence on his reliability. What relationship does the narrator have in fact to the characters and events he portrays? Is he 'a stalwart proponent of the dominant ideology' in German society in 1974, or 'not entirely devoid of sympathy and compassion' (RK 15) for Katharina? Is the narrator's stance really dispassionate? In fact, an objective and accurate account of events must prove unattainable, however conscientious the narrator: the selection and arrangement of material cannot be accomplished without subjectivity playing a role. In his important interview with Böll, Manfred Durzak has complained that the anonymity of the narrator impedes the reader in this respect. In the absence of information regarding the narrator's personality, attitudes and goals, the reader struggles to ascertain when and where these factors interfere with his depiction of the 'facts'. Tellingly, faced with these criticisms, Böll must admit that 'ziemliche Schwächen' (MD 329) mark his use of a narrator. Initially, he dismisses these weaknesses as unimportant, as part of a transitional learning phase in his work, but, in the end, he concedes more freely: 'Vielleicht wars einfach ein Irrtum von mir, überhaupt einen Erzähler einzubauen' (MD 330).

Such considerations have not prevented some critics from discerning a development in the relationship between the narrator and the characters and events he portrays. Rhys Williams has identified 'the abandonment of narrative neutrality' within the 'Bericht': 'What begins [...] as a dispassionate account becomes a highly sympathetic and partisan exoneration of Katharina's behaviour' (RW 56). Philip Payne even goes as far as to wonder whether the internal narrator suppresses vital evidence, whether he comes to forget his 'oath of objectivity' (PP 45)? This critic's doubts arise because the narrator does not divulge the contents of a telephone conversation—recorded by the police—between Katharina and Ludwig. Payne seems to have overlooked, however, details offered in the 'Bericht' of strict regulations regarding the use of tape recordings as evidence (K 86-87). The narrator may not have had access to such recordings; at one point he expresses the (presumably unfulfilled) longing: 'Könnte man doch die Tonbänder mal vorspielen lassen!' (K 89). The general point made by Williams and Payne about lack of neutrality further underlines, nevertheless, how difficult it is to make definite statements about the reliability of the narrator. Consequently, the reader must be careful when formulating any conclusions, based on the narrator's version of events, about the case of Katharina Blum. This technical difficulty inevitably affects every interpretation of this complex text.

The 'Erzählung'

We can now turn our attention from these aspects of the narrator's 'Bericht' to the form of Böll's 'Erzählung'. *Die verlorene Ehre der Katharina Blum* can be viewed, on this higher level, as a demonstration of the different possibilities of literary and journalistic texts. Certainly, as a linguistic presentation of the events surrounding Katharina, Böll's 'Erzählung', with its ability to reflect the complexities of the situation, and engage the interest of the reader, easily betters the salacious coverage of the same incidents by the gutter press. Literature enjoys several advantages not automatically available even to quality journalism. Firstly, the independence of the author means that he need not fear pressure from newspaper proprietors to espouse a political system or ideology in his writing; his own subjectivity and personal choice can thus play a larger role. Secondly, the creative writer does not face the daily or weekly deadlines which journalists must meet. This greater flexibility with regard to the gestation period of his works means that insights have more time to evolve, a fuller overview of his subject matter can be attained and reflected; whereas journalism must often content itself with a snapshot, literature can thus offer more readily a well thought-out and carefully composed picture. Thirdly, literature permits the writer to tackle a theme in an endless number of ways, whereas the journalist must bear in mind the physical constraints of the actual newspaper, as well as the stylistic decrees of the editors and the expectations of the readers. Fourthly, literature allows more scope for an inventive imagination. The form and style of *Die verlorene Ehre der Katharina Blum* benefit from such advantages.

The author's selection of a literary genre is significant since this choice foresees for the work not a short-lived existence, but a certain timelessness in terms of its validity. Böll may not write consciously 'für die Ewigkeit'. He may even claim modestly, 'Es ist mir gleichgültig, ob irgendeiner nach meinem Tod sich noch für irgend etwas interessiert, was ich geschrieben habe' (E2 552). Such statements, however, detract in no way from the fact that a literary text, by its very nature, benefits inevitably from 'Ewigkeits-Faktoren'.[1] Of course, a literary text can sink into oblivion, but such an occurrence might normally be traced back to the weaknesses of the work in question, or to its regrettable neglect by the critics and reading public, whereas a more expendable, intrinsically ephemeral form actually characterises journalistic writing. Literature possesses a greater 'Ewigkeitswert'.[2] In *Die verlorene Ehre der Katharina Blum*, it remains unclear whether the narrator's 'Bericht' represents a journalistic document or a dossier designed for more private use. In either case it would be inexorably linked with day-to-day life and might be rendered useless by the next day's newspaper, or be consigned to dusty files or a shredding machine. Böll's 'Erzählung', on the other hand, published and translated world-wide, received and continues to receive the attention of innumerable readers and critics.

How does the form of *Die verlorene Ehre der Katharina Blum* compare with traditional literary genres? Interestingly, this 'Erzählung', composed in the last third of the twentieth century, can be considered to feature characteristics typical of the Novelle, that German literary tradition which was particularly prominent in the nineteenth century. The murder of Tötges might well meet with the expectations of Goethe's well-known definition, formulated in conversation with Eckermann in January 1827: 'denn was ist eine Novelle anders als eine sich ereignete unerhörte Begebenheit?';[3] certainly, the press views Katharina's (fictional) murder of Tötges as an outrageous occurence ('unerhörte Begebenheit'). Similarly, given that the ZEITUNG represents, on one level, an all-pervading force which impinges, now overtly, now insidiously, on all realms of human existence, this newspaper might be regarded as a distinctive symbol; as such, Böll's text would comply with Paul Heyse's famous 'Falkentheorie'—i.e. with the formal requirement for the Novelle to feature a symbolic 'Falke' (literally: 'falcon/hawk'). The 'Erzählung' likewise includes a 'Wendepunkt' ('turning-point'), albeit one which proves difficult to identify: the question of exactly when Katharina took the decision to kill Tötges remains open. Moreover, as is typical of many Novellen, Böll presents his story through the perspective of a narrator. In traditional Novellen, the author often creates a narrative framework ('Rahmenerzählung') within which the actual tale ('Binnenerzählung') is told. The narrator in *Die verlorene Ehre der Katharina Blum* may not entertain an audience at a hearth or camp-fire, but he nevertheless shapes and articulates the story. In terms of length, too, Böll's 'Erzählung' resembles the Novelle.

It is interesting to measure this work against the tentative definition of the genre offered by John Ellis: 'It has been agreed that the Novelle deals with a single event, and one which is of a striking character (i.e. 'headlines' material)'.⁴ In *Die verlorene Ehre der Katharina Blum,* Böll seeks to fathom Katharina's murder of Tötges, demonstrating by means of this single example 'wie Gewalt entstehen und wohin sie führen kann' (K 3); moreover, the involvement of the ZEITUNG means that the 'Erzählung' deals with 'headlines' material' in the most literal sense. Ellis continues his definition: 'The striking event makes for a narrative with a rather clear outline, and one which is sharply focused; this means that it is in its composition artistically concentrated'; Böll's 'Erzählung' focuses sharply on the period from 20 to 24 February 1974 which culminates in Tötges's death. John Ellis concludes: 'Because the event is so central, character is less important in the Novelle, and there is little or no development of character'; *Die verlorene Ehre der Katharina Blum* depicts in any depth only the development in the heroine 'from conformity to rebellion',⁵ the narrator's brief comments on the numerous secondary figures amount to mere sketches. To this extent, Böll's 'Erzählung' from the year 1974 fits Ellis's definition of the nineteenth-century genre, the Novelle.

Not surprisingly, however, since at least a century separates Böll's 'Erzählung' and the well-known Novellen of the nineteenth century, *Die verlorene Ehre der Katharina Blum* moves beyond the conventions of the older literary form—hence the revealing subtitle of Margit Sinka's essay on the book as a *Novelle:* 'or How a Genre Concept Develops and Where It Can Lead'.⁶ Böll, writing in the 1970s, is inevitably influenced by the narrative possibilities evolved by such writers as James Joyce (1882-1941) and Franz Kafka (1883-1924) earlier in the twentieth century; the narrative strategies of his 'Erzählung' would be unimaginable without the developments, achieved by such major literary figures, in modern fiction. Nor should we overlook the fact that by the time of the publication of his 'Erzählung', Böll had been cultivating his own prose forms for at least thirty years. Likewise, evidence exists in the text of a strong impression made by the documentary literature prevalent in West Germany in the late 1960s and early 1970s. As Hans-Gerhard Winter has discussed in detail, 'Dokumentarliteratur' focused on documents as a source of material about historical and social conditions, on verifiable objective truths as opposed to the subjective impressions of the author; writers tried to intervene more directly in political matters, and showed, correspondingly, a much reduced emphasis on psychological development and aesthetics. Winter himself has noted the mark left by 'Dokumentarliteratur' on Böll's writing: 'Die Autoren der älteren Generation erweisen diesem Trend der Zeit [...] durchaus ihre Reverenz: Heinrich Böll mit *Katharina Blum* (1974), einer Erzählung in fiktiv dokumentarischer Form, die an die Erfahrungen des Autors mit der Springerpresse anknüpft'.[7] The proximity of Böll's 'Erzählung' to documentary literature should not, however, be overstressed. *Die verlorene Ehre der Katharina Blum* may incorporate statements and documents from various sources, but it does not operate without the powers of imagination, inventiveness, and an interest in the psyche of individual characters. Thus, Böll's 'Erzählung', while it reflects both the major trends of twentieth century fiction and the achievements of thirty years of the author's own writing, also represents, to this degree, a certain assertion against the then more recent developments in German literature, against the documentary literature of the immediately preceding ten years. Böll did not share the view of the younger generation, led by Hans Magnus Enzensberger (born 1929), who maintained in 1968 that literature was dead, that no place remained for literary fiction.

The Individual: Katharina Blum

Why does Heinrich Böll draw the attention of his readership in the 1970s, and in the years to come, to an ordinary woman, living and working in West Germany in 1974, with the inconspicuous name Katharina Blum? Why does he elevate this largely unremarkable woman to the status of a representative figure by putting the spotlight on her in the very title of his book? To be sure, the author even goes as far as to establish a link between his fictional figure and the German literary tradition within which he writes: in the eighteenth century, Friedrich von Schiller (1759-1805) completed a story called *Der Verbrecher aus verlorener Ehre* (1785). What entitles Katharina Blum to be associated with such a lofty, indeed classical, concept as 'honour' ('Ehre')? Why the modifier 'lost' ('verloren'), which suggests a tragic and irreversible fate? Clearly, the (at first sight) unlikely importance which Böll attributes to this un-extraordinary woman represents a direct challenge to the reader to consider carefully the fate of this figure.

Katharina Blum attains unwanted prominence when, in 1974, the gutter press presents a distorted image of her. Her chance encounter with Ludwig Götten, a deserter from the 'Bundeswehr', and above all his escape from the police while in Katharina's company, expose this young woman to an extreme form of public suspicion which is nurtured by the near-hysterical response of West German society to the activities of the Baader-Meinhof group. Katharina's brief contact with Götten inspires the ZEITUNG to portray her as a 'Räuberliebchen' (K 32) and 'Mörderbraut' (K 35), as 'eine in jeder Beziehung radikale Person' (K 38), as 'eiskalt und berechnend', as having 'eine richtig nuttige Art' (K 101). Even her modest flat is suddenly suspected of being 'ein Konspirationszentrum, ein Bandentreff, ein Waffenumschlagplatz' (K 33). Such sensationalist reporting represents a gross distortion which has grave consequences for Katharina—as summarised rather colourfully by the blurb of a translation published in America: 'Paraded across the front pages of a big-city newspaper, portrayed as a whore, an atheist, a communist sympathizer, she becomes the target of anonymous phone calls and letters, sexual advances and threats' (MR 257). It is in response to such newspaper reports that Böll's narrator begins, in his 'Bericht', to piece together a more balanced and accurate assessment of the woman.

Katharina's lack of qualifications for the role imposed on her by the ZEITUNG soon transpires from the sources quoted by the narrator. This twenty-seven-year-old, renowned for her 'ordnende Hand' (K 74), is anything but a terrorist or anarchist. Her curriculum vitae, formulated during her first interrogation and recorded in section 15 of the 'Bericht', tells a tale of rags to modest and well-earned riches—and thus, on another level, reflects the economic history of post-war West Germany. The poverty of Katharina's early years parallels the more general hardship in Germany immediately after World War II; indeed, when Katharina (born on 2 March 1947) is six years old, her father dies of a lung injury sustained during the war. Katharina leaves school at fourteen, works as a maid, domestic and housekeeper, attends courses to gain qualifications in this realm of work. By 1970, her dedication and conscientious attitude to work, coupled with her caution in money matters, enable her to move into her own appartment. Katharina's progress, underpinned by traditional German values, has a certain parallel in the Restoration and Economic Miracle achieved in the Federal Republic after the deprivation of the immediate post-war period. To this extent, Katharina would seem to be a conformist, an exemplary member of society who poses no political threat to her community. Tellingly, in 1968, that important watershed year for West German social attitudes, Katharina—who in that year reaches the symbolic age of twenty-one—does not become involved in the student movement, but instead aims for further professional progress, and prepares to settle down in (an ultimately unsuccessful) marriage. She remains, as Moray McGowan comments, 'virtually untouched by the attitudinal, behavioural and sartorial changes ushered in by the student movement and the youth revolt of the 1960s'.[8] That the ZEITUNG should present Katharina as a radical extremist in 1974, seems, given this evidence, all the more ironic.

Katharina's attitude to work and her disinclination to be active politically show her publicly to espouse the values of her society. As a private individual too, she behaves in a manner which suggests her unsuitability for the role attributed to her in the Götten affair by the gutter press. In sexual matters, Katharina has the reputation of being rather reserved, indeed her prudishness earns her the nickname 'die Nonne' (K 47). Similarly, her Christian name means 'the pure one', her surname 'flower'. Böll has insisted, however, that he does not regard Katharina as a saintly figure, as an example for others to follow. The author emphasises, for example, that her keenness to work might equally be interpreted negatively. For Böll, Katharina is a 'lädierter Engel'.[9] We should not overlook that she becomes guilty of complicity when she assists Götten to escape by sharing with this lawbreaker her knowledge of the various passageways in the basement of the appartment block. Such details suggest that Katharina may not be as conservative as she might appear at first sight.

Katharina Blum does place her society in question in other ways. She may not plant bombs or raid banks, but she does not conform in that she is childless, divorced, and no longer a member of any church. Her ability to survive without the support of a male partner successfully challenges society's norms too. Her marriage failed after just six months partly because of her husband's lack of respect for her person, as reflected in the manner in which he invaded her private space: Katharina reports, 'der sei eben nie zärtlich, sondern immer zudringlich gewesen' (K 27). Rather than tolerate such behaviour, Katharina asserts her independence, protects her personal rights. She aims too for financial independence, hence her reluctance to accept too much support from the Blornas. Her habit of going for long, otherwise pointless drives also illustrates her individualism. It is Katharina's 'sprachliche Sensibilität' (K 39), however, which challenges society's values most powerfully in that it exposes the dubious assumptions on which norms are based. Katharina practises a form of linguistic resistance throughout her interrogations at police headquarters, for she intuits, rightly, 'how language determines perceptions of reality and simultaneously conditions social interaction' (MR 264). These various traits underline the considerable extent of Katharina's individualistic nature; inevitably, she clashes with the Establishment, as represented by the police, the church and the press. Her honour, her reputation, may be destroyed in the process, but, equally, the Establishment does not acquit itself well. This ironic twist makes the title of Richard Kilborn's monograph—*Whose Lost Honour?* (RK 1)—particularly apt.

The Police

The activities of the police prove much more striking in the visual images of the film *Die verlorene Ehre der Katharina Blum* than in Böll's original book. The most memorable scene depicts how masked and armed men, hardly recognisable as police officers, indeed looking more like terrorists, storm Katharina's appartment. This dramatic and traumatic incident is intercut most effectively with contrasting shots of Katharina's ordinary preparations for breakfast. The young woman, supposedly innocent until proved guilty, later experiences rough treatment at the hands of the police both when she is escorted away for interrogation and while in police custody. Such violence stands in ironic contrast to the gentleness and tenderness displayed towards Katharina by the alleged hardened terrorist Ludwig Götten. It is not Böll's intention, however, to focus in a one-sided way on the question of police brutality. Indeed, it would be inappropriate to view Katharina's encounters with the police as a simple confrontation between a 'goody' and 'baddies'. The issue is much more complex: ultimately, the role played by the police causes us to question not only the methods employed by the individual officers involved, but also the mentality of the nation, of the State, on whose behalf the force operates.

Böll's presentation of the police in *Die verlorene Ehre der Katharina Blum* gains in effectiveness by virtue of its differentiated nature. As well as instances of cruel behaviour, of unfair treatment, Böll depicts individual officers whose attitudes and actions do not reflect the reputation earned for the police force by other less conscientious colleagues. The narrator characterises the approach of the woman officer Pletzer as 'wohlwollend' (K 24). Moeding, Beizmenne's assistant, even earns the ironic suggestion of his superior that he, Moeding, has fallen in love with Katharina when he suggests that she should be held in custody for her own protection; Moeding goes as far as to advise Katharina not to make or accept telephone calls, nor to read the newspapers the following day, though these two pieces of advice may have cost him—personally—dearly, or endangered the lives of his colleagues (K 30-31). Even Beizmenne, an irrational character who at times treats Katharina harshly, is shown, with a degree of sympathy, to be susceptible and at the mercy of his own moods. That Katharina does not represent the most cooperative of detainees becomes clear in the course of the interrogations too; her apparent pedantry, her fussy demands regarding exactness, and her refusal to expose other individuals in order to protect herself, all cause her interrogators much frustration. A fairer image of the police thus emerges. Moreover, Böll's ability to hint at the individual psyches of the people involved, rather than portray merely an impersonal encounter between a detainee and her stereotype interrogators, has the added advantage for the reader of conveying the various interesting tensions, the intriguing minor dramas which arise between the protagonists.

Böll may not paint the police completely black, but he does question certain of their tactics seriously. The issue of police observation, of surveillance, worries the author deeply, so much so that his next book, *Berichte zur Gesinnungslage der Nation* (1975), again concerns itself with police methods; in this often hilarious satire, Böll contrives a situation in which snoopers engage in mutual snooping! Similarly, the later novel *Fürsorgliche Belagerung* (1979) which shows how security cameras, installed for protection, come to dominate and impede the lives of a prominent family, presents—in this symbolic form—what Böll has called 'die Gefangenschaft der Überwachten und der Bewachten' and 'die Übergänge zwischen überwacht und bewacht'. Böll counts these issues among the most important and topical phenomena and problems of present times, not just in the Federal Republic of Germany, but internationally: 'Die Menschen werden ja auch durch die Bewachung zerstört'.[10] No doubt it is difficult to strike the necessary but delicate balance between the use of 'Überwachungsmethoden' (K 77) to fight serious crime and terrorism, and thus protect both individuals and society, on the one hand, and the danger of abuse of the same measures, on the other. Inevitably, such surveillance means that the private sphere of the individual is violated in some way; in the worst instances, such violations can even represent 'a constant infringement of the individual's right to privacy and to freedom of movement and association' (RK 46).

Interestingly, in *Die verlorene Ehre der Katharina Blum,* Böll pinpoints the problematical implications of such working methods not just for those people under observation, but also for those individuals employed to 'observe'. In witty, satirical passages, he includes some disconcerting speculations as regards the effect of such work on the psyche of the officers involved. Section 42 of the 'Erzählung' highlights the possibility of discussions about Lüding's favourite desserts being interpreted as an anarchist code (!), and wonders about possible detrimental effects suffered by telephone tappers whose innocent ears are subjected to everything 'zwischen Karamelpudding und härtestem Porno' (K 90). This section not only illustrates Böll's great gift for satire so apparent in other works; it emphasises too the voyeuristic aspect of police surveillance.

The conspiracy with the press represents another aspect of police activity strongly criticised by Böll. The author can in fact point to personal experience as the victim of such collusion: by October 1977, homes of his family were raided four times. On the ARD news programme 'Tagesthemen' of 4 October of that year, Böll declared: 'Ich habe den Beweis, daß die Springer-Presse mit der Polizei zusammenarbeitet'; Springer sprang to its own defence with a denial broadcast on 18 October but, as the newsreader added, pointedly, its biggest newspaper in Berlin, the *BZ,* had somehow (!) managed to report on 7 February 1974 about a 'Hausdurchsuchung beim Sohn des Nobelpreisträgers Heinrich Böll'—although the raid took place only in the afternoon of the day on which this morning newspaper appeared.[11] This (in retrospect) entertaining anecdote would seem to offer some evidence of a conspiracy between the police and the press. In the film *Die verlorene Ehre der Katharina Blum,* no doubt remains: the cinema spectator actually witnesses meetings between Beizmenne and Tötges, and their exchange of documents and information. The reader of the 'Erzählung', on the other hand, has to invest more effort in personal detective work to establish that certain details which come to light during interrogations later find their way into press reports.

The first textual evidence of this conspiracy lies perhaps in the presence of press photographers when the police arrest Katharina Blum (K 19). Ironically, Katharina herself later asks the police of all people for protection against the press; she finds it 'unbegreiflich' (K 54) that details discussed during the interrogations—for example, the matter of her 'Herrenbesuch'—should have become available to the press. Only after the arrest of Ludwig Götten does Beizmenne admit openly to an association with the newspaper world; Beizmenne goes as far as to express his gratitude to reporters employed by the ZEITUNG whose 'lockere und nicht immer konventionelle Methoden' (K 103), unavailable to honest police researchers, uncovered helpful facts. Böll's criticism is that the trading of such information—for the press does not volunteer its material for free—infringes the individual's right to confidentiality when questioned by the police. Again ironically, this conspiracy between the police and the press operates while Beizmenne hounds Katharina, in search of evidence for his 'Theorie von einer Verschwörung, in die Katharina verwickelt sei' (K 30), and for his suspicion that her flat represents a 'Konspirationszentrum' (K 33).

It transpires that the police contribute to Katharina's troubles in another serious way: their deliberate delaying tactics in the matter of arresting Ludwig Götten make possible in the first instance her chance encounter with this man. Had the police arrested Götten at the earliest opportunity, Ludwig and Katharina might never have met. By later choosing once again not to arrest Götten, but to surround Katharina's flat while he sleeps there, the police incur some guilt with regard to his escape, and thus also to the character assassination to which the ZEITUNG subsequently subjects Katharina. Unknown to the young woman, the police place her home under surveillance, tap her telephone conversation with Ludwig, and eventually surround the villa of Alois Sträubleder—Götten's refuge—for almost forty-eight hours before arresting their target. Beizmenne justifies these delays in terms of his objective of observing Ludwig's attempts to contact his fellows, whom the police eventually arrest too. The fact remains, however, that while Beizmenne indulges in a tactical delay, events develop in Katharina's life which have horrific repercussions. While Beizmenne uses her as bait, allowing her to roam freely in the hope that she might lead him to her 'Herrenbesuch' and/or Götten, Katharina incriminates herself, the press persecute her, and events leading to her murder of Tötges gather momentum. Moreover, Beizmenne's rather cynical toying with the lives of individuals does not represent the action of one irresponsible officer: the Minister for the Interior is fully informed throughout and in agreement with the measures taken. This approval at ministerial level shows the State to be similarly guilty of such shabby and sinister treatment of individuals.

Such police tactics attribute to the officers concerned the role of gods, as it were, who from a lofty and privileged position observe the actions of mere mortals as they incriminate themselves. The police officers portrayed in Böll's book, however, are neither omniscient nor omnipotent nor the unsullied upholders of unlimited virtues. This police force does not have the capacity to identify and enforce — independently of various external pressures — some objective notion of law and order, of right and wrong. Instead, in the historical context of a near-hysterical political climate generated by West German society's reaction to the activities of the Baader-Meinhof group, the population and its legal representatives fall prey to a witch-hunt mentality. Tellingly, when in Schlöndorff's film it is suggested that Götten will be sentenced to eight to ten years of imprisonment, the implication is that not some fair and objective penal code, but the prevailing hysteria, will determine the length of the sentence.

Böll's 'Erzählung' represents an accomplished depiction, characterised by great understanding, of a police force, manned by ordinary human beings having to operate in trying times in West Germany. The British reader will recall the unenviable pressures faced by the police in Northern Ireland in the 1970s and 1980s, or during the miners' strike in the mid 1980s. Readers of other nationalities may no doubt find (near-)parallels in their own societies. Böll's clear underlying beliefs can be related to every society. Democratic countries must protect themselves against the emergence of a police state which would suppress and oppress civil liberty. When responding to a terrorist threat, society must therefore be careful not to swing towards 'the progressive curtailment of civil liberties' which, for Böll and Schlöndorff, would form 'a far more severe threat to society than supposed 'terrorist' subversion' (RK 44). The individual must likewise be protected against the situation, described by the American Mark W. Rectanus when he writes on Böll's book, in which 'the rules of the game are established by the police and the media who themselves can overstep boundaries without invoking societal sanctions' (MR 264). In short, the police force must never be permitted to become 'an organisation far more concerned with enforcement and suppression than with the rights of the subject against intimidation and injustice' (RK 47). One major merit of *Die verlorene Ehre der Katharina Blum* lies in its ability to alert the individual reader to such dangers and, by extension, to recommend him/her to guard against such developments in society; as such, Böll actively encourages his readers to contribute positively to the democracy in which they may have the good fortune to live.

The Church

Heinrich Böll found reason throughout his lifetime to be critical of the Catholic Church as an institution. In the last decade of his life he finally took the step of officially leaving the Church, of depriving it of his 'Kirchensteuer' ('Church Tax'). He continued, though, to cherish the fundamental principles of Christianity; as Joachim Kaiser suggested in his obituary on the author, Böll 'lashed out against Catholicism ... not because he was un-Catholic but undoubtedly because he was too Catholic' (OD 19). The writer sought 'a society based on a kind of primitive Christianity, simple, unsophisticated, erected on a few basic principles: on love, gentleness, pity, mercy, reverence and mutual respect'.[12] Before examining the depiction of the Church in *Die verlorene Ehre der Katharina Blum*, we should therefore first consider the author's criticisms of this powerful institution.

Böll deplored the official reaction of the Catholic Church to certain key historical developments in Germany. He condemned above all its inadequate response to the Third Reich, in particular the fact that during the reign of Pope Pius XI (1922-1939), Eugenio Pacelli, later to become Pius XII (1939-1958), engineered a concordat with Hitler: 'Nach Machtübernahme, Reichstagsbrand,

Märzwahlen [1933] erhielten die Nazis ausgerechnet vom Vatikan ihre erste internationale Groß-Anerkennung'.[13] In short, as discussed too in the controversial play *Der Stellvertreter* (1963) by Rolf Hochhuth (born 1931), Roman Catholicism failed to offer active resistance to Fascism. Significantly, two events in 1987 rekindled interest in this issue. Firstly, during a pastoral visit to West Germany in May, John Paul II made Church resistance to the Nazi regime the dominant theme of his visit by beatifying both a Jesuit priest and a Jewish born nun and philosopher; this Pope's more positive assessment of the Catholic response to National Socialism was seen by some critics, however, as 'an attempt by the Catholic Church to re-write history by singling out a few Catholic officials who publicly condemned the Nazis'.[14] Secondly, the Vatican's decision to invite the Austrian President Kurt Waldheim to visit the Holy City in June 1987 strained its relations with the Jews who denounced the meeting between the Pontiff and the President as a justification of Nazi atrocities; the visit occurred at a time when Waldheim's alleged Nazi past—especially his role as an officer of the Wehrmacht in the Balkans during World War II—was the subject of the world-wide protests of anti-Nazi and Jewish organisations.[15] Clearly, Böll's criticism of the Church's failure in the face of National Socialism remains topical even in the late 1980s.

The author likewise condemned the position adopted by the Catholic Church in post-war German society. In Böll's view, its close association with the Christian Democratic Union (CDU) amounted to support for the forces of materialism and capitalism. A church thus geared towards wealth and social power, a church which is the bedfellow of the Establishment, fails in its duty to the individual, neglects his more basic and spiritual needs. As a result of its vested interests, the Church fails too in the public, political sphere. Enid Macpherson has reported how 'in 1955 when the question of the re-creation of the German army was raised, the main point that occupied the consideration of the Church was the form and quality of the prayer book which should be issued, not the moral issue as to whether West Germany should have an army at all'.[16] In *Ansichten eines Clowns* (1963), a novel written from the perspective of the clown Hans Schnier, Böll's first-person narrator attacks the narrow-minded intolerance, the uncritical conformist and bourgeois attitudes, and the cynical snobbishness characteristic of certain Catholic circles in West Germany, including, ironically, would-be progressive groupings. Schnier's existence collapses in the face of the hypocrisy displayed when prominent Catholics persuade his wife, Marie, to abandon him for one of their number. Böll illustrates in this novel—which earned him, unfairly, the charge of 'Anti-katholizismus'—how 'katholische Luft' can choke individuality.[17]

In *Die verlorene Ehre der Katharina Blum,* the Church does not play such a central role as in previous works by Böll. Katharina, like the author, leaves the Church, in her case at the age of nineteen (K 41). Her former husband, as quoted by the ZEITUNG, even charges her—unjustly—with 'Kirchenfeindlichkeit' (K 37). For Katharina, churches merely represent buildings where she can find tranquillity. During one interrogation, she indicates that she visits churches 'nicht aus religiösen Gründen, sondern weil man da Ruhe hat'; single women, she instructs the police, are less likely to be harassed in churches than in cinemas. Typically, following her murder of Tötges, Katharina twice visits a church, not to pray or seek forgiveness, but 'weil das an diesem Karnevalssonntag der einzige Ort war, wo man ein bißchen Ruhe fand'(K 121).

In Böll's book, the Church plays relatively little direct part in Katharina's predicament. In Schlöndorff's film, on the other hand, Dominican monks conspire to arrange a meeting between Katharina and her 'Herrenbesuch', Alois Sträubleder. Ironically, according to the 'Erzählung', Sträubleder is attending a 'Tagung für christliche Unternehmer'—as the main speaker and chairman of a 'Grundsatzdiskussion'!—when news of Katharina's arrest first spreads (K 34). This leading Christian entrepreneur not only deceives his wife and abandons Katharina when controversy breaks out, he also conspires selfishly to protect his own public image; as such, Sträubleder is hardly the best ambassador for Catholicism. In the original 'Erzählung', the Church features in Katharina's life mainly in the past. Again ironically, the Church that likes to say 'Love Thy Neighbour' shares, indeed perpetrates, the prejudices of society at large, especially towards Communism. Katharina's father is dismissed as 'ein verkappter Kommunist' (K 106) on the strength of one comparatively innocuous statement: 'Der Sozialismus ist gar nicht das schlechteste' (K 107). When in 1974 Blorna investigates the accuracy of comments attributed to the local clergyman by the ZEITUNG, this supposedly religious man reiterates his discriminatory remarks about Herr Blum's Communism; he lacks concrete evidence, but claims that his sensitive nostrils could detect the political persuasions of Katharina's father. The same priest had teased Katharina at school, calling her 'unser rötliches Kathrinchen'

(K 121). Such details show the caring, sharing Church to be as biased
and bigoted as other sections of society. Moreover, when Dr.
Blorna tries to question these attitudes critically, the intolerant and
unenlightened priest reminds him, yet more sinisterly, of his
'Gehorsamspflicht' (K 107), of his duty as a Roman Catholic to
display unquestioning obedience to the Church. Accordingly, *Die
verlorene Ehre der Katharina Blum* presents the Church, ideally the
source of solace, comfort, and spiritual strength for the individual,
as one more uncaring institution which stifles, or even persecutes,
ordinary human beings.

The Press

There are lies, damned lies, and gutter press reports. This
variation on the well-known quotation would seem to sum up Böll's
assessment of popular journalism in *Die verlorene Ehre der
Katharina Blum*. The author's personal experiences at the sometimes
dirty hands of West German newspapers provide the background to,
but not the sole motivation for, his presentation of the press in this
piece of fiction. As widely recognised, Böll was the victim of a
smear-campaign launched in the early 1970s by the Springer press,
and by the BILD-Zeitung in particular. In his 'Erzählung' published
in 1974, Böll allows no doubt as regards the principal target of his
condemnation of journalism: in a statement preceding the main text,
he asserts: 'Sollten sich bei der Schilderung gewisser journalistischer
Praktiken Ähnlichkeiten mit den Praktiken der >Bild<-Zeitung
ergeben haben, so sind diese Ähnlichkeiten weder beabsichtigt noch
zufällig, sondern unvermeidlich' (K 5). Such undisguised criticism
has not escaped critics. Indeed, the American Mark W. Rectanus has
suggested that 'public knowledge of Böll's articles regarding the
Baader-Meinhof Group, as well as his criticism of the Springer Press
and the *Bild-Zeitung,* provided the basis for widespread media
recognition of the book in the Federal Republic' (MR 254). Rhys
Williams has gone as far as to argue that 'a skirmish with the BILD-
ZEITUNG appears to be as helpful to the career of a German
novelist as a prosecution of PRIVATE EYE is to a British politician'
(RW 57). Typically, however, Böll's unambiguous slating of the
press is not one-sided and unqualified. Just as his critical portrayal of
the police benefits from the depiction of exceptions in the form of

some positively fair officers, so the recognition that not all newspapers indulge in character assassination strengthens the case against the ZEITUNG in the 'Erzählung'; some, like the *Umschau* (a disguised reference to the *Frankfurter Rundschau*?), report 'in durchaus sachlicher Form' (K 55).

Die verlorene Ehre der Katharina Blum, Böll's 'literarische Auseinandersetzung mit dem Sensationsjournalismus',[18] highlights undesirable flaws at every point on the newspaper production line. The first stage, the investigative endeavours of journalists, comes under attack. Böll condemns, as discussed more fully earlier, the reporters' collusion with the police. Moreover, the reporter Tötges and his photographer colleague, Schönner, are shown to employ 'lockere und nicht immer konventionelle Methoden' (K 103) which are unavailable to police researchers whose tactics are presumably monitored more closely and, if necessary, penalised. It is suggested, for example, but not with complete certainty, that Tötges, disguised as a painter and decorator, managed to interview Katharina's mother shortly after her major operation for cancer; and that his action of confronting Frau Blum with certain 'facts' regarding her daughter's arrest contributed significantly to her premature death (K 91-3). In the 'Erzählung', violent murders punish 'the manipulative, sensation-seeking, distorting practices that are the stock-in-trade of the popular (Bild-Zeitung) journalist' (RK 50): Katharina Blum shoots Tötges; Adolf Schönner is found dead in a wood (K 10). Böll clearly disapproves of their approach to the journalist's task.

The deaths of these two newspaper employees do not, however, bring about the abandonment of their methods. Böll's narrator indicates that Eginhard Templer, the 'Nachfolger' of Werner Tötges, practises 'eine Art Fortsetzung von Tötges' (K 111); and that Herr Kottensehl, Schönner's successor, photographs Blorna when he hits Alois Sträubleder at the opening of an art exhibition (K 115). This self-perpetuating nature of the profession represents one worrying feature of investigative journalism highlighted by Böll. Richard Kilborn has pointed to a second such aspect: 'in many ways the methods and practices of the 'newsgatherers' bear a clear resemblance to the surveillance techniques and procedures employed by the police authorities' (RK 52). Thirdly, it becomes apparent from the 'Erzählung' that no location exists where the individual might be safe from such journalists and newspapers. On a skiing holiday, Dr. and Frau Blorna are accosted by an employee of the ZEITUNG at their winter resort. Trude Blorna comments, so the narrator reports, 'diese Pest verfolge einen in die ganze Welt, nirgendwo sei man sicher' (K 74); her husband similarly curses 'diesen Dreck, diesen verfluchten Dreck, der einen über die ganze Welt hinverfolgt' (K 75). Böll's serious reservations about the methods of newspaper reporters are underlined when his initially reticent narrator becomes explicit and outspoken in his criticism of the press for fear that 'bloße Andeutungen' might be overlooked or misinterpreted (K 104).

The author condemns, too, aspects of the next stage in the newspaper production line: the composition of articles in the popular press. Extracts from the ZEITUNG on the case of Katharina Blum are presented in italicized passages (K 32-3; 35-8; 100-102). Philip Payne has summarized these reports very neatly: '*DIE ZEITUNG* exemplifies journalism at its most sordid: it is a despicable mix of unsubstantiated assertion, half-truth enhanced by rumour, sexual innuendo and pandering to the secret desires and secret fears of a worldly-wise yet gullible readership' (PP 48). The narrator's quotation of extracts permits the reader to measure their content against the 'truth' as documented elsewhere in the 'Erzählung'. It soon transpires that newspapers cannot live by truth alone; the lying goes from strength to strength. Journalists distort statements given by Katharina's acquaintances in good faith. Blorna's description of Katharina as 'eine sehr kluge und kühle Person' is twisted to present her as 'eiskalt und berechnend' (K 32); his general comments regarding the individual and crime are misreported in such a way as to portray Katharina as 'durchaus eines Verbrechens fähig' (K 33). Similarly, Dr. Berthold Hiepertz, who had stated: 'Wenn Katharina radikal ist, dann ist sie radikal hilfsbereit, planvoll und intelligent—ich müßte mich schon sehr in ihr getäuscht haben'; and who pointed to his long experience and usual accuracy in the assessment of individuals; finds his appraisal of Katharina misquoted as 'eine in jeder Beziehung radikale Person, die uns geschickt getäuscht hat' (K 38). Not even the words of Katharina's dying mother are recorded accurately: the despairing questions 'Warum mußte das so enden, warum mußte das so kommen?' are rendered as statements, implying a less ambiguous acceptance of Tötges' version of events—'So mußte es ja kommen, so mußte es ja enden' (K 91). The journalist shows no regard for the effect of such distortions on the relationships between Katharina and the individuals (mis)quoted.

Several other negative characteristics of such newspaper reports can be discerned. Emotive language is used to unleash fear, suspicion and hate in readers. Headlines present Katharina as a 'Räuberliebchen' (K 32) and 'Mörderbraut' (K 35); reports portray Ludwig Götten as a 'Bandit und Mörder' (K 33), as 'blutbefleckt' (K 101). The deliberate association of Katharina, her family and friends with certain taboo subjects in the oversensitive hysteria of the Federal Republic represents another feature of these reports. Katharina's father, 'ein verkappter Kommunist' (K 33), is condemned for his Communist views. The provocative presentation of his wife brings together the themes of sex and religion: it is claimed that she stole Communion wine and celebrated orgies with her lovers in the sacristy of the local church (K 33). Similarly, the appraisal of Katharina given by her estranged husband, Wilhelm Brettloh, is jaundiced by its juxtaposition with emphatic references to his tears, and with allusions to the (supposed) respectability, honesty and modesty of this ordinary working man who does not trust trade unions. For the reader of the ZEITUNG, Brettloh thus stands in stark contrast to Katharina who, according to her ex-husband, entertains false notions about socialism, radical views, and hostile feelings towards the Church (K 37). Further suspicions are aroused regarding her relative wealth and rapid rise professionally. It is insinuated that Katharina's associations with people of left-wing political persuasions may have assisted such progress (K 37, 101). In the absence of evidence, as an alternative to sheer invention, reporters pose leading, or rather: misleading questions which they leave unanswered. Such queries regarding Katharina's father, her brother, her professional advancement, and her relationship with the Blornas do not give the individuals concerned the benefit of the doubt until answers can be found. Instead, the cunning phrasing of such questions and the context in which they appear encourage negative verdicts. Böll has elsewhere described this reporting style as 'die typisch faschistische, indirekte Art—nur so eben, daß man's riechen kann' (E2 556). The combined effect of all these stylistic strategies can ruin the lives of innocent individuals; Katharina therefore classes the offending journalists as 'Mörder und Rufmörder' (K 94).

Given the above, it is especially ironic that the ZEITUNG should stress so often its desire to present the reader with facts, with 'unumstößlichen Fakten' (K 37); and that it should lie repeatedly about supposed unceasing endeavours to keep its readers fully informed about key developments (K 36-7). *Die verlorene Ehre der Katharina Blum* illustrates how newspapers, despite their duty to inform the public by publishing factual material, prefer instead to print money in the form of sensationalised stories which sell well. Even more sinisterly, with their falsified version of events, the journalists attempt to fashion the perception of Katharina Blum by the public, and perhaps even by the police and courts. The SONNTAGSZEITUNG points out that Katharina is still at large, 'immer noch auf freiem Fuß' (K 100), in a way which constitutes a thinly disguised plea for her arrest. Such inappropriate intervention in judicial matters becomes more overt when the editors wonder, not for the first time but 'zum wiederholten Male': 'sind unsere Vernehmungsmethoden nicht doch zu milde? Soll man gegen Unmenschen menschlich bleiben müssen?' (K 101-102). When it is appreciated that some ten million readers consume such writings daily, these editorial policies seem yet more appalling.

When the finished newspaper leaves the production line, the public buys and reads that edition. Böll focuses on the dangers which can attend this final stage of the process too. However badly written, however economical with the truth, newspapers of this ilk influence the judgement of its readership, affect its perception of reality. This frightening connection is mirrored throughout the 'Erzählung': a taxi driver recognises the Blornas from the ZEITUNG and comments, in terms which reveal the extent of the influence, 'Sie sind doch der Anwalt und Arbeitgeber von diesem Nüttchen' (K 36); Käthe Bekering of the Cafe Bekering seems to believe at least some of what she read in the press (K 122); Katharina's hate mail includes cuttings from the ZEITUNG which presumably aroused the senders' aggressive sentiments (K 69). The narrator emphasises, rather condescendingly, that 'relativ rationale Menschen' fall prey to the ZEITUNG too: Dr. Heinen initially regards Katharina as a Marxist because of the newspaper reports (K 94-5); when Blorna learns of the content of the SONNTAGSZEITUNG, he threatens to attack both the newspaper offices and Alois Sträubleder's home with Molotow Cocktails. Blorna's reaction underlines for the narrator 'wie sogar gebildete und etablierte Menschen empört waren und Gewalttaten gröbster Art erwogen' (K 106). The dangerous effect on public opinion clearly should not be underestimated.

Heinrich Böll, when himself the victim of a smear campaign in the 1970s, could fall back on his solid position as an established author. In Britain in 1987, the best-selling pulp novelist and former political figure, Jeffrey Archer, could draw upon sufficient personal resources to defend himself against allegations in *The Star* that he had sex with a vice girl. In Böll's 'Erzählung', Alois Sträubleder, in the face of press coverage of his association with Katharina, succeeds in using his wealth and contacts to protect his career and reputation. These three examples—from West Germany, Great Britain and fiction— underline how prominence, power, and financial strength can act as a buffer against a press campaign and remove some fear of forbidding legal costs. Böll's literary focus on Katharina Blum, on the other hand, underscores a key point: the average individual does not necessarily have the resources to withstand such a vicious onslaught on his/her reputation. In fact, an interest in 'what happens to a completely unknown defenceless person who through some chance or other hits the headlines' (RK 25) motivated Böll to write *Die verlorene Ehre der Katharina Blum*. The character assassination endured by Katharina underlines all the more strikingly the need for a balance to be restored between individual privacy and public information.

The case of Katharina Blum illustrates how difficult it is to uphold the freedom of the press, on the one hand, and to guard the rights of the individual, on the other. The press seems the better able to fend for itself. 'Irrsinnige Aufregung. Schlagzeilen. Titelblätter. Sonderausgaben. Todesanzeigen überdimensionalen Ausmaßes' (K 12) mark the trade's response to the murder of Tötges and Schönner. Böll's narrator who highlights such 'Über-Aufmerksamkeit der Presse' considers that Tötges was buried 'mit einem unangemessenen Aufwand' (K 13). The treatment of Tötges's funeral in the film version of *Die verlorene Ehre der Katharina Blum* proves particularly effective. In the hard-hitting epilogue, a parody of the hypocritical sanctimoniousness and self-righteousness of the press, a leading representative of the ZEITUNG uses the occasion of the death of Tötges, this 'Opfer seines Berufes' (K 13), to hold a grand-sounding speech in praise of press freedom. Ironically, the cinema audience realises that his words form a satirical and unambiguous indictment of everything represented by the Establishment, for the speech praises the very machinery which, once in motion, soon destroyed the reputation of Katharina Blum. Moray McGowan has pinpointed this telling irony: 'anti-social and anarchic behaviour may be generated by the very organs of society that claim to stand for order'.[19] Similarly, Mark W. Rectanus has usefully highlighted how, in public life, the media contributes to the formulation of 'the rules of the game' but can itself 'overstep boundaries without invoking social sanctions' (MR 264). For Rectanus, the fate of Katharina Blum demonstrates, moreover, how 'the press masks its own overt political interests by politicizing an apolitical event' (MR 264). By employing Katharina as an unfortunate scapegoat in order scathingly to attack the political viewpoint which she allegedly represents, so the ZEITUNG by implication consolidates or even strengthens the position of its own politics in the eyes of the public. In short, the press normally commands significantly more power than the individual and can abuse that advantage.

Such discussion of press irresponsibility should not divert attention away from the question of the responsibility of the individual reader. Millions of Germans still read the *BILD-Zeitung* today, still consume what Böll has colourfully called 'Springer-Polit-Porno-Krimis' (E2 575), despite the author's literary and more polemical protests, and despite significant exposures in the documentary reports published by his friend and colleague, Günter Wallraff. [20] Philip Payne's summary of the purport of Böll's 'Erzählung' has thus lost none of its potency: 'Böll understands that it is not simply legislation that is needed but a change of attitude and, even more, a change of heart; he sees it and he shows it, forcefully, persuasively and imaginatively in *Die verlorene Ehre der Katharina Blum*' (PP 54). If, despite Böll's efforts, newspapers are in fact responding to the needs and wants of its readership; if they are pandering to public prejudices, to a dependence on scandalous gossip; then the individual must confront his own, private culpability for the inadequacies of our press.

Language

Given that Böll's narrator presents *Die verlorene Ehre der Katharina Blum* in the form of a written report, and that it focuses on the journalist profession and the nature of newspaper articles, it is no surprise that language should emerge as one major theme. Richard Kilborn, in a neat summary of the breadth of language actually employed in the 'Erzählung', praises its 'wide cross-section of contrasting styles and registers, ranging from the dry, unemotional prose of the police statement to the lurid journalese of the gutter press, from the 'straight' reproduction of character dialogue to the more general philosophical musings or conjectures in which the narrator himself is occasionally wont to indulge' (RK 18).

Böll's text, moreover, both raises interesting questions regarding various aspects of language, and illustrates the very concrete implications for everyday social intercourse between human beings of such (at first sight) abstract considerations.

For historical reasons which should not be overlooked, German authors of Böll's generation command a particularly acute linguistic awareness. Alfred Andersch, in typically understated terms, has outlined the crucial importance of language for any writer: an author operates in a 'Sprach-Welt', language represents his 'Arbeitsmaterial'; a writer thus works constantly 'mit seinem Sprach-Instinkt und seinem Sprach-Bewusstsein'.[21] German authors such as Andersch and Böll, however, who grew to maturity during the Third Reich, had first to overcome a major obstacle before they could use language to write creatively: the linguistic tradition into which they had been born and which they would have inherited normally had been despoiled and debased by the rhetoric and euphemisms of the Nazis. In Andersch's third novel, *Efraim* (1967), the hero—a journalist who, in the course of the book, moves increasingly towards a more literary form of writing—discusses how the German language suffered during the Third Reich, how it acquired 'the evil eye': Efraim observes 'how the survivors—with the exception of a few politicians—are always biting their tongues and how literature tries to get along without metaphors'.[22] Heinrich Böll managed, nonetheless, to develop a pride in his own language: 'Wenn Sie monatelang als fucking German Nazi behandelt werden und in den Hintern getreten, dann denken Sie, [...] ich bin trotzdem Deutscher, und ich werde schreiben'.[23] For Böll, Andersch and other members of the 'Gruppe 47'—a loose association of writers instigated in 1947 by Hans Werner Richter (born 1908), and key actors, it was to turn out, in the rehabilitation of German language and literature after 1945—post-war writing was to become, in Böll's own words, 'eine Literatur der Sprachfindung',[24] '[eine] Suche nach einer bewohnbaren Sprache in einem bewohnbaren Land'.[25] Böll and his contemporaries confronted the task of a critical reappraisal of the German language. Writers thus sensitized to the connotations and implications of individual phrases were especially well qualified to assess developments in the idiom of German after World War II. In *Die verlorene Ehre der Katharina Blum,* Böll, equipped with his sharp awareness of the recent history of the German language, endeavours to enhance the 'Sprach-Instinkt' and 'Sprach-Bewusstsein' of his readers.

Böll's motive for tackling this vital task lies in his 'precise analysis of how language determines perceptions of reality and simultaneously conditions social interaction' (MR 264). He realises that language employed to describe reality may, by means of its associations and tone, colour the individual's view of that reality. Language can be used unscrupulously to manipulate and distort truth; examples of this phenomenon abound, as discussed earlier, in the extracts from the ZEITUNG reproduced in the 'Erzählung'. Any such distortion has serious political consequences, for the individual's perception of reality shapes his actions in the public sphere of life. Language can affect relations between individuals too, as Böll shows. Katharina Blum refuses energetically to use the crude verb 'ficken' with reference to her love-making with Ludwig Götten; if, as suggested in the text, Beizmenne did in fact ask during one interrogation: 'Hat er [Ludwig] dich denn gefickt?' (K 18), then it is more than plausible that this phrase unleashed bitterness, fury and a sense of humiliation in Katharina and consequently destroyed any possibility of a mutual trust between the police officer and his detainee. Similarly, when the journalist Tötges arrives for an exclusive interview with Katharina, he addresses her condescendingly with diminutive forms of her surname—'Blümchen', 'mein Blümelein'—and employs the equally crude verb 'bumsen' to propose sexual intercourse with her; Katharina, offended, responds by shooting Tötges and thinks—tellingly—'Gut, jetzt bumst's' (K 120). Böll's female characters seem especially sensitive to language. Trude Blorna, too, for example, can guess the identity of Katharina's male visitor accurately, assisted by a linguistic distinction: she holds that only Alois Sträubleder can be the 'Herrenbesuch', for Ludwig Götten—given his background and type—would more likely be described as a 'Männerbesuch' (K 75). Trude's deliberately ironic use of 'Herrenbesuch' later strains relations between the Blornas and Sträubleder (K 85). These few representative examples underline how the narrative of *Die verlorene Ehre der Katharina Blum* illustrates the concrete implications for human affairs of semantic considerations.

Language, in that it reflects the consciousness of the speaker and thus mirrors the deep-rooted attitudes and leanings of both individuals and society as a whole, can be an indicator of underlying inhumane sentiments which might easily become concrete instances of inhumanity. A way of speaking betrays a way of thinking—which, in turn, might be translated into a way of behaving towards others. For Eberhard Scheiffele, Böll's use in the 'Erzählung' of colloquialisms, i.e. the language of the ordinary German, serves to demonstrate 'wieviel verborgene Wertsetzung, wie viele Urteile, wieviel Aggressivität, wieviel autoritäres Denken in dieser angeblich 'wertneutralen', 'pluralistischen', 'offenen' Gesellschaft virulent sind'. [26] Everyday language can thus record instances of bias; common usages can function as markers for certain trends and tendencies, for 'the verbal violence of society' (RW 55). Scheiffele, having read Böll's 'Erzählung', discerns even more clearly 'Tendenzen des Integrierens oder Ausschließens, Verächtlich-machens, Verteufelns'[27] in everyday German. language, we might conclude, can both re-affirm in the user's mind and communicate to a listener feelings of violent aggression and discrimination.

When, during interrogations, Katharina Blum insists on the deletion of inappropriate words from the police record and on their replacement with more accurate and less loaded terms, her efforts thus do not represent mere pedantry; rather, such 'regelrechte Definitions-kontroversen' (K 26) form part of a battle to protect her identity and integrity. Katharina is not handicapped by inarticulateness; she does not require the 'Artikulationshilfe' (K 92) which Tötges so cynically affords her dying mother. This individual does not take on board in a passive and uncritical fashion the idiom of the linguistic culture in which she operates, for actively to use such expressions would be to appear to endorse them in all their implications. Instead, Katharina intuitively challenges the underlying values and norms. Such sensitivity to language might be regarded as the surface reflection of some deep-seated political instinct in the individual. In turn, such instinctive responses could be nurtured to become a firm political consciousness which, subsequently, might provide the basis for concrete political action. For these reasons, it is all the more important for the individual to sharpen and maintain linguistic awareness, to resist any stultifying developments in society's attitudes to, and use of, language. Katharina's exemplary 'sprachliche Sensibilität' (K 39), deep-rooted and far-reaching, thus forms the precious basis for a strong challenge which might be mounted by the individual within a social context.

Violence

The important subtitle of *Die verlorene Ehre der Katharina
Blum* underlines the prominence given to the theme of
'Gewalt' — 'violence' or 'force' — in this work. Böll states without
equivocation his intention to investigate 'Wie Gewalt entstehen und
wohin sie führen kann' (K 3). Authors of Böll's generation, we
should note, experienced at first hand especially violent periods in
German history. As a result, Böll's presentation of 'How violence
develops and where it can lead' (KT 3) in 1974 is informed by an
awareness of the wrestling for political power in the Weimar
Republic; of the horrors and atrocities of the Third Reich, the
concentrations camps and World War II; of the violent scenes which
attended the student movement in 1968; and of the terrorist activities
of the Baader-Meinhof group in the early 1970s.

The curious lack of active resistance faced by the National
Socialists when they seized power in 1933, and in the years which
followed, was a phenomenon long to engage the minds of Böll's
generation. One author in particular, Böll's contemporary, writer
colleague, and personal friend, Alfred Andersch, highlights this
absence of forceful opposition in his autobiographical writings.
Critical of the inadequate response of the German Communist Party
(KPD) to the rise of Fascism in the early 1930s, Andersch suggests
that it should have declared a civil war: 'Ein deutscher Bürgerkrieg
hätte der Welt einen Weltkrieg erspart./ Stattdessen liess die Partei
sich geschlossen in die Konzentrationslager treiben, wie eine Herde
Schafe in den Pferch'.[28] This failure of the Communist Party, of
tragic consequence for German, European, and world history,
occupied Andersch even in the late 1970s, not long before his death
in February 1980.

Whereas the National Socialists' rise to power met with little
resistance in Germany, violence and force, perverse in nature and
extreme in degree, characterised the Third Reich which followed.
Böll has testified to the subsequent 'Straßen-Brutalität, wo Leute
einfach zusammengeschlagen und verhaftet und weggeschleppt
wurden, nicht nur Fremde, auch Freunde...' (CL 54). When
conscripted to the army, Böll then experienced at first hand the
horrors of World War II in France, the Soviet Union, Rumania,
Hungary and Western Germany. In the immediate aftermath of the
war, at the very latest, his generation was informed about the

atrocious crimes against humanity committed in the concentration camps. Böll emphasises that the violence of Fascism, of the Third Reich, of World War II, did not cease with the end of hostilities in 1945; its physical effects linger on, thinking and feeling human beings—as individuals and members of society—must come to terms with it. This aspect of continuity illustrated for Böll 'daß der Krieg niemals zu Ende sein würde, niemals, solange noch irgendwo eine Wunde blutete, die er geschlagen hat'.[29] Such insights, derived from personal experience and thus a heightened awareness of such extreme forms of violence, formed the basis of attempts by the post-war generation of writers to ensure that similar events should never recur.

Recur they did nevertheless—or at least: one significant school of thought insists that a Fascist renewal took place in West Germany in the 1950s. Alfred Döblin (1878-1957), exiled from Germany during the Third Reich, spent the years 1953-1956 mainly back in France, having identified in the Federal Republic a 'braune Pest, die heute anders auftritt als unter Adolf [Hitler]'.[30] The letters of Alfred Andersch and Arno Schmidt (1914-1979) reflect a similar perception of political developments in Adenauer's Germany.[31] Böll, for his part, has identified a 'first wave of intimidation'—the second was to follow in the 1970s—against the opposition at this time: 'Die erste erfolgreiche Einschüchterungswelle, die Anfang der fünfziger Jahre an- und Ende der fünfziger Jahre auslief, ist mir noch gut in Erinnerung; es war eine großangelegte Intellektuellen- und Kommunistenhatz' (E2 577). For left-wing intellectuals, the debate surrounding rearmament and remilitarization in the 1950s showed that reactionary tendencies were still prevalent in the country. Former Nazis continued to occupy positions of power in industry and government. Caution, indeed censorship, was practiced in the cultural sphere. Revealingly, the years under the chancellorship of Konrad Adenauer have become known as the Restoration: old political values were restored, an opportunity for important social change was squandered. Too few lessons had been learned from the not so distant past .

In the late 1960s, the student movement exposed evidence of remnants of the Nazi era and aimed to correct the consequent errors made by West German society in the short history of the Federal Republic. As we discussed in our examination earlier of the years 1967-1977, however, violence marked this process too. Indeed, Alfred Andersch has highlighted the 'Gewalt-Problem' and the

element of 'Linksfaschismus'[32] associated with the students as
reasons, among others, for the critical distance he maintained from
the movement. Böll, too, qualified his sympathy and support for the
APO with frequent statements against the use of violence. To
compound the problem, the social and political backlash against the
student movement, as against the terrorist threat in the 1970s, took
on violent qualities also. When Böll presented *Die verlorene Ehre
der Katharina Blum* in 1974, violence represented not only a burning
issue in West German society but also a social ill with widespread
implications. In his literary portrayal of the causes and harmful
effects of this phenomenon, a depiction qualified by his direct
experience in Germany throughout four or five decades, Böll takes
an unambiguous stance against violence.

It is thus all the more incredible that *Die verlorene Ehre der
Katharina Blum* should have been called 'an armchair celebration of
someone else's violence' (MR 260); and that Böll himself has been
denounced as one of the 'Großväter der Gewalt'.[33] Heinrich Jokodus
Lummer of the CDU in Berlin made the latter claim in 1974 when
he refused to attend a reception in honour of Böll and Helmut
Gollwitzer. A few weeks earlier, on the evening of the funeral of the
Berlin judge Günther von Drenkmann who was shot by terrorists,
Matthias Walden, in a commentary on ARD television, counted Böll
among those people who had fertilized 'den Boden der Gewalt ...
durch den Ungeist der Sympathie mit den Gewalttätern'.[34] The
author won a legal case against Walden after eight years. Such
charges were serious, for legislation in Germany, in the form of
'Paragraph 88a', expressly forbids the glorification of violence.

Böll's critics were very much mistaken. *Die verlorene Ehre der
Katharina Blum* does not seek to justify violence; the 'Erzählung'
aims rather to examine 'how violence develops and where it can lead'
(KT 3). The finished text thus does not condone violence and force,
but serves instead as an indicator of the symptoms of violence and as
a warning against the danger it represents. In conversation with
Christian Linder, Böll asserts: 'Die Darstellung von Gewalt [ist]
keine Rechtfertigung von Gewalt' (CL 88); and explains further:
'Wenn ich einen Mord schildere, rechtfertige ich ihn doch nicht,
sondern stelle nur die Menschen in ihren Konflikten dar' (CL 90).
This distinction between a mere depiction, on the one hand, and the
active justification of violence, on the other, may seem clear and
unproblematical to readers today. In the immediate aftermath of the
publication of the 'Erzählung' in 1974, however, the political climate

and the thrust of public opinion obscured the judgement of many German readers, such that Rhys Williams observed in 1979: 'English readers of the novel might well be puzzled by the vehemence of the reaction to a book which ostensibly does not deal with terrorism at all' (RW 50). To be true, Böll neither condones the murder of Tötges, nor does he identify with Katharina Blum: 'Bei einem solchen Stoff und bei einem wie dort geschilderten Verbrechen wollte ich natürlich auf keinen Fall Identifikationen verursachen' (MD 330). Indeed, faced with Linder's interpretation that Katharina shoots Tötges to restore her lost honour, Böll even goes as far as to insist that she cannot regain her integrity by means of such an act of revenge: 'Ich finde es auch richtig, daß sie nicht integer bleibt' (CL 67).

Die verlorene Ehre der Katharina Blum in no way exonerates violence. Böll does concede, however, that no author can anticipate what his work might unleash in the mind of a reader, or what consequence the act of reading might have for the individual's subsequent actions: 'Das Gefährliche ist—und das muß wirklich jeden Autor beunruhigen—daß er nicht weiß, was er mit jedem Buch, jedem Film, jedem Theaterstück in Bewegung stezt; denn das ist ja nicht kontrollierbar; und das ist wirklich problematisch' (CL 84). Too little research has been completed on the reading process; it is not possible to measure its effect on the individual's consciousness and behaviour. Writers, who might be held to bear a certain guilt or responsibility for their readers' actions, need therefore proceed with care when they practice their art. At the same time, literature would be unimaginable without depictions of violence. Böll points to such seminal works as *The Old Testament*, Homer's Greek epic poem *Odyssey*, the medieval *Nibelungenlied* and Camus's *L'Etranger* (1942), and underscores the irony 'daß fast alle geistigen Quellen des Abendlandes Gewaltverkündungen sind' (CL 85). Böll prefers the notion of 'Konflikt' to that of 'Gewalt', and defines: 'Literatur [...] stellt nun einmal Konflikte dar' (CL 87). He justifies depictions of such conflicts in his works with the (should-be) commonplace: 'Es entstehen eben Spannungen, Konflikte, Probleme, die Gewalt hervorrufen, im Leben und in der Literatur' (CL 90). We can be confident that an author so sensitive to 'wie geistige Gewalt sich in körperliche Gewalt umsetzt' (CL 89), will deal conscientiously with delicate issues.

Böll's responsible stance towards the treatment of violence extends to an attempt to increase the public's awareness of existing violence, to sensitize society to the more insidious forms of violence. Böll stresses that society has failed adequately to define the notion of 'Gewalt': 'Was heißt Gewalt? Wir haben, das ist vielleicht das Bedauerliche, Gewalt noch nicht bis auf den Grund definiert' (CL 89). By neglecting this task, society hampers its own capacity to deal with instances of violence in daily life. Böll, for his part, endeavours to assist society towards a more enlightened, more differentiated definition of 'Gewalt'. At a conference of the SPD in Dortmund on 12 October 1972, Böll emphasised the topicality of the theme, before commenting: 'Stillschweigend hat man sich darauf geeinigt, unter Gewalt nur die eine, die sichtbare zu verstehen: Bomben, Pistolen, Knüppel, Steine, Wasserwerfer und Tränengasgranaten. — Ich möchte hier von anderer Gewalt und anderen Gewalten sprechen' (E2 605). The author proceeded to highlight, for instance, the force or violence exerted in the pursuit of profit, and that practised in banks and stock exchanges. In 1975, the author again made this distinction between 'visible' and 'invisible' violence: 'Gewalt ist ein großes, ein zu großes Wort; es deckt zu viel, und meistens denken wir nur an Bomben und Pistolen, nie an die, die sie herstellen, verkaufen; und wir vergessen auch, daß diese Art von Gewalt möglicherweise die Entladung oder Entsicherung unsichtbarer Gewalt ist: mag sie nun persönlich, psychologisch, oder system- oder strukturbedingt sein' (CL 87). Böll's definition of 'violence' embraces far more than just revolting students and terrorist gangs. His central concern is the devaluation of human life which violence entails: 'Und wieviel Lebenswertes wird durch all diese Gewalten, die unseren Alltag kommandieren, verhindert, deformiert, gefälscht?' (E2 606). Such attitudes show Böll to be no nihilist, no terrorist, but a man who abhors violence.

Numerous critics have pinpointed different types of violence condemned by the author. As Philip Payne has discerned, 'Böll shows . . . that violence is not the preserve of terrorists but can start in the offices of a large newspaper' (PP 53); in his speech to the SPD Conference in 1972, Böll had spotlighted 'die massive publizistische Gewalt einiger Pressekonzerne' (E2 605). Böll perceives too, as discussed earlier, 'the potential for language to become a medium of aggression' (MR 259). Moreover, as J.H. Reid has claimed in his essay on the author's later novel, *Fürsorgliche Belagerung* (1979), 'Böll implies that, abhorrent as the terrorists may be, their terrorism is matched by that of the conservative forces in society. As in *Katharina Blum* he shows violent intolerance in the population at large'.[35] Such awareness and presentation of these various forms of violence support Rhys Williams' contention that the subtitle of *Die verlorene Ehre der Katharina Blum* 'acquires an ambiguity': 'The violence signifies both Katharina's character assassination and Tötges's literal assassination. The subtitle also suggests that Böll is at least as concerned with the processes at work within the police and the press as he is with what happens next' (RW 51). Böll's wider definition and more differentiated depiction of 'Gewalt' represent his contribution towards attempts to restrict violence in society.

The restrained tone of the depictions of the major violent incidents in *Die verlorene Ehre der Katharina Blum* also overthrows the charge that the 'Erzählung' constitutes 'an armchair celebration of someone else's violence' (MR 260). The internal narrator does not glorify or dramatize violence in the manner of the blood-thirsty, sensation-seeking gutter press, but insists instead that only a minimum of physical violence should be portrayed (K 79). With more than a hint of irony, Böll has his narrator aestheticize and so almost anaesthetize his description of the murdered Tötges:

> Es soll hier nicht so viel von Blut gesprochen werden, [...], und deshalb wird hiermit aufs Fernsehen und aufs Kino verwiesen, auf Grusi- und Musicals einschlägiger Art; [...]. Vielleicht sollte man lediglich auf gewisse Farbeffekte hinweisen: der erschossene Tötges trug ein improvisiertes Scheichkostüm, das aus einem schon recht verschlissenen Bettuch zurechtgeschneidert war, und jedermann weiß doch, was viel rotes Blut auf viel Weißes anrichten kann; da wird eine Pistole notwendigerweise fast zur Spritzpistole, und da es sich im Falle des Kostüms ja um *Leinwand* handelt, liegen hier moderne Malerei und Bühnenbild näher als Dränage (K 9-10).

When the narrator concludes this extravagant description (the written equivalent of a multi-media show?), and the section of his report in which it appears, with the much more down-to-earth comment 'Gut. Das sind also die Fakten' (K 10), Böll's irony is unmistakable. The narrator, with his extended poetic license, has embellished the facts, if in a manner quite different from that of the ZEITUNG; the style of the resulting passage, however, will not offend the German reader hyper-sensitive to the theme of violence, as might have done a more sober, realistic account.

Much more disturbing are the often understated depictions of the harmful effect of violence—'visible' and 'invisible', overt and insidious—on individuals. The premature death of Katharina's mother, precipitated by Tötges' brutal intrusion on her convalescence with devastating 'facts' about her daughter, attracts the ironic commentary of the narrator: 'Der Tod der Frau Blum wurde zwar gewaltsam herbeigeführt, aber unbeabsichtigt gewaltsam' (K 90-91). Sections 51 and 52 of the 'Erzählung' report on the deleterious effect of events on the careers of the Blorna couple; Dr. Blorna's decline and his increasing neglect of his person are eventually symbolized by his body odour (K 111). Violence as perceived and experienced by Else Woltersheim, Katharina's godmother, friend and confidante, causes 'eine sich steigernde Verbitterung' and 'verstärkte gesellschaftsfeindliche Tendenzen' (K 114) to grow in this woman. Negative developments in Katharina, set in motion by her subjection to 'visible' and 'invisible' violence, culminate in her murder of Tötges, but her 'Verstörtheit' and loss of interest in her appartment marked earlier signs of her deterioration (K 56). Such small but intimate details of the effect on the individuals concerned combine to form the strongest indictment of the forms of violence highlighted in the 'Erzählung'.

In *Die verlorene Ehre der Katharina Blum*, Böll does in fact offer an alternative to 'Gewalt' which has been largely overlooked by readers and critics. Böll, who introduced the notion of 'Gnade' to the public debate about Ulrike Meinhof in 1972, promotes 'Zärtlichkeit' ('gentleness' or 'tenderness') in his 'Erzählung' two years later. The term first features prominently in the text when Katharina insists during one interrogation that the word 'Zudringlichkeiten', and not 'Zärtlichkeiten', be used in police records to describe the advances made to her by gentlemen at the Blornas' parties (K 27). This distinction soon proves to be no mere foible on Katharina's part. The difference is even 'von entscheidender Bedeutung' for her: her former husband's tendency always to be 'zudringlich', not 'zärtlich', became one reason for their separation (K 27). In the course of the 'Erzählung', the noun 'Zärtlichkeit' acquires yet more importance. Tenderness typifies the relationship between Katharina and Ludwig Götten: through him, with him, and in him, Katharina discovers, and manages herself to express, gentleness. Götten, an outlaw and murderer according to the gutter press, proves to be 'so lieb', to possess 'große Zärtlichkeit' (K 51). Indeed, Böll's narrator presents the couple in very positive terms as 'Zärtlichkeitsempfinder' (K 51). In the film *Die verlorene Ehre der Katharina Blum*, the lovers' tenderness is, for obvious reasons, much more visible, and is tellingly juxtaposed with portrayals of police violence. In the book, Böll contrasts, by implication, the wholly positive connotations of the word 'Zärtlichkeit' for the lovers, on the one hand, with its degradation in the context of obscene telephone calls and letters to Katharina, on the other. One caller, later named 'der Zärtlichkeitsanbieter' (K 87), proposes some form of sexual gymnastics to Katharina, claiming to be 'bereit und in der Lage, ihr jede, aber auch jede Art von Zärtlichkeit zu bieten' (K 67). Katharina likewise receives a 'Zärtlichkeitskatalog', produced by a firm which supplies sex articles, and bearing the hand-written remark, 'Das sind die wahren Zärtlichkeiten' (K 69). This clearly deliberate and structured stress on the notion of 'Zärtlichkeit' becomes lost, most inappropriately, in the English translation of the 'Erzählung' which is inconsistent or completely remiss when the contrastive usage should be rendered (KT 64,66).

The telling emphasis on 'Zärtlichkeit' acquires added significance when we consider this strand of the text alongside comments made by the author in March 1975. In conversation with Christian Linder, Böll identifies 'eine Theologie der [...] Zärtlichkeit' (CL 72) in the *New Testament*. This phenomenon appeals, by its very nature, greatly to the author: it is ' [eine] Zärtlichkeit, die immer heilend wirkt: durch Worte, durch Handauflegen, das man ja auch Streicheln nennen kann, durch Küsse, eine gemeinsame Mahlzeit' (CL 72). Böll proceeds to express his regret that this aspect of the *New Testament* has never found full echo and permeated daily life, but has instead been obscured and obstructed by a harmful stress on dogma, principles and catechisms: 'Dieses Element des Neuen Testaments—das zärtliche—ist noch gar nicht entdeckt worden; es ist alles in Anbrüllen, Anschnauzen verwandelt worden' (CL 72). Opportunities have been missed, in Germany too. For Heinrich Böll, the Federal Republic represents 'eine(s) der unzärtlichsten Länder'; he invites his interviewer to imagine instead a 'sozialistische Zärtlichkeit' (CL 72)—which neither man attempts to define. Regrettably, Böll's remarks remained fragmentary. A much fuller presentation of the author's thinking on this matter would have been helpful. Coupled with the positive presentation of Katharina Blum and Ludwig Götten as 'Zärtlichkeitsempfinder' (K 51), however, even these fragments suffice to suggest that Böll cherished a personal 'Theologie der Zärtlichkeit'—one easily reconcilable with his emphasis in 1972 on the notion of 'Gnade' ('mercy'), and with his rejection of the alternative which would mean living 'gnadenlos, in Schlagzeilen und mit Pistolen, gnadenlos dumm, gnadenlos faschistisch, gnadenlos demagogisch' (E2 557). The West German society in which Böll lived and worked, on the other hand, feared in

the 1970s that violence—'Gewalt'—threatened its very existence.
Ironically, that same society did not perceive that in the controversial
and much-maligned 'Erzählung' *Die verlorene Ehre der Katharina
Blum* its Nobel Prize-winning author had sketched the beginnings of
a blueprint for its survival.

Conclusion

Die verlorene Ehre der Katharina Blum treats of politically contentious issues, all acutely relevant to the specific historical context in which Böll wrote and set the 'Erzählung': the roles of the police, Church, press, and violence in society. Indeed, the response of West German society to the fictional figure Katharina Blum in 1974, a response which touches upon each of these issues, resembles, in its manifestations and motivation, that faced in reality in Germany by the student movement and the Baader-Meinhof group. The particular historical experience of the Third Reich, the political upheaval of the late 1960s, and the terrorist threat of the early 1970s, conditions the reaction portrayed by Böll. Nevertheless, the judgement, expressed in a review in *The New Yorker* , that 'the people and the institutions in the story are uniquely and unmistakably German' (MR 259) could not be more fallacious. The American reviewer does a grave injustice to the wider implications of the narrative. On one level, for example, with its focus on 'complex social mechanisms' (MR 259), on the manipulation of truth, and on the constellations of power in everyday public life, Böll's text depicts 'the price the individual has had to pay for the establishment of a modern society' (KB 246). It is therefore the aim of this concluding section to demonstrate that *Die verlorene Ehre der Katharina Blum* can be interpreted on levels too which transcend time and place.

Viewed in general terms, Katharina Blum, like Schiller's hero, the 'Sonnenwirt', in *Der Verbrecher aus verlorener Ehre,* written almost two centuries earlier, may be seen as 'the average human being exposed to the stresses of existence'.[1] In everyday life, the individual can find himself confronted with the rigours of reality, with the exigencies of a situation not of his creation, and which he cannot appraise fully. *Die verlorene Ehre der Katharina Blum* delineates, as the internal narrator indicates, the 'unglückseligen Verstrickungen einer völlig unbescholtenen Person' (K 55). Böll emphasises the dangerous aspect of 'Getriebenwerden in eine bestimmte Ecke' (MD 330) in such a desperate predicament: circumstances can (seem to) trap the individual, permitting no scope for free choices, decisions and action. Tellingly, the author had likewise stressed this notion of 'in die Enge getrieben' (E2 543) with regard to the Baader-Meinhof group in 'Will Ulrike Meinhof Gnade oder freies Geleit?' (1972). What Buttler, in Act IV,8 of Schiller's

Wallensteins Tod, terms 'die feindliche Zusammenkunft der Dinge',
can thus even force the individual, in such circumstances, to incur
guilt. Katharina might well sympathise with the frustration and
inability to comprehend life expressed by Max in Act III,18 of the
same play:

> Und eine Frevelhandlung faßt die andere
> In enggeschloßener Kette grausend an.
> Doch wie gerieten wir, die nichts verschuldet,
> In diesen Kreis des Unglücks und Verbrechens.[2]

Early in life, Böll himself had experienced a similar sense of
'Ausgeliefertsein': at the time of the economic collapse of Germany
in the late 1920s, and again during the Nazi era, the Böll family felt
frighteningly powerless, at the mercy of developments in the
political sphere, 'völlig hilflos ... gegenüber diesen Umständen'.[3]
Such powerlessness finds expression in *Die verlorene Ehre der
Katharina Blum* too. In all these ways, the 'Erzählung' represents an
impressive literary portrayal of the complex circumstances, the
entanglements, in which the unsuspecting individual can become
inextricably embroiled in daily life.

Die verlorene Ehre der Katharina Blum illustrates too the
perennial problem of the conflict between the rights of the private
individual, on the one hand, and the demands of the public realm of
life, on the other. The narrator records how developments in
Katharina's life in February 1974 clash with the mood of the public
as engendered by the Carneval. One organiser complains that news
of the death of Tötges and Schönner might have spoiled the festival
atmosphere and ruined a good business opportunity (K 11-12).
Similarly, a fellow guest objects to the seriousness which
immediately characterises Katharina's relationship with Ludwig
when they first meet at a party: 'Das habe dem Abend einen Ernst,
fast etwas Feierliches gegeben, das zu karnevalistischen
Veranstaltungen nicht so recht passe'(K 63). Of course, on another
level, Katharina's interrogation by the police likewise gives rise to
tensions between her right to privacy and society's right to
investigate crime. It becomes clear that Beizmenne's question
regarding the unexplained 25,000 kilometres recorded on the
mileometer of her car touches upon 'ein intimes Geheimnis der
Blum' (K 43); Beizmenne's dogged pursuit of details not always
relevant to her association with Götten impinges repeatedly upon
Katharina's 'Intimsphäre' (K 45). Press coverage of the case,

supposedly satisfying the public's right to information, proves intrusive in similar fashion. When Katharina complains to the police about reports, Staatsanwalt Hach insists, however, that through her involvement with Ludwig, she has become public property, 'eine "Person der Zeitgeschichte" und damit Gegenstand berechtigten öffentlichen Interesses' (K 54); when Tötges later wishes to interview Katharina's critically-ill mother in hospital, he protests to the doctor in charge that she too is a 'Person der Zeitgeschichte' (K 91). The interests of the press and the individuals concerned vary considerably. This conflict crosses all borders.

Die verlorene Ehre der Katharina Blum underlines too the difficulty of accurately recording facts, of describing objective reality. Not just complex motives and complicated sequences of events defy definition, even comparatively straightforward statistics are open to misinterpretation. Despite the detailed nature of the police records of Katharina's interrogations, despite her insistence on 'Ausführlichkeit' (K 25), these statements—like the narrator's 'Bericht'—are ultimately deficient, even though they do not distort facts in the manner of the ZEITUNG. Böll's 'Erzählung' thus illustrates a general observation made by his German-Swiss contemporary, Max Frisch (born 1911): 'Facts as such never declare themselves. We always manipulate them, and it is impossible to cover all of them. A computer could do it but in that case nothing would be expressed any more. The selection of facts already means interpretation, representing an intent'.[4] *Die verlorene Ehre der Katharina Blum* also expresses how even inanimate objects can provide the basis for misinterpretation: the expensive ring given to Katharina by Sträubleder—her 'Herrenbesuch' whom she refuses to identify—arouses the suspicion of the police. Similarly, objects can take on a new aura or significance in the light of events, as developments in Blorna's reaction to his study (K 79-80) and Katharina's perception of her appartment (K 56) show. Language, too, can acquire additional connotations in these circumstances: Sträubleder's dubious role as gentleman visitor, his guilt and uncertainty about this relationship, and his consequent indirect involvement with Götten, have the effect that the word 'Herrenbesuch' becomes 'ominös' (K 85), 'neuralgisch' (K 99), for him. These various strands of the narrative combine to make Böll's 'Erzählung', on one level, a powerful parable of the unattainability of objective truth.

The response of literary critics to the works of Heinrich Böll has

long featured—alongside the superlatives and unstinting praise—a
nagging doubt: is Böll really a good writer? Even when he was
awarded the Nobel Prize for Literature in 1972, a commentary in
the *Times Literary Supplement* conceded: 'There are excellent
political and personal reasons for the award', yet asked: 'But what
about Böll's literary stature?'[5] Jochen Vogt has acknowledged 'Bölls
Schwächen als Schriftsteller'.[6] Marcel Reich-Ranicki has admitted:
'We do not know if his novels will still be read in the next century'
(OD 13). *Die verlorene Ehre der Katharina Blum*, in particular, did
not meet with the unanimous approval of the critics. In this case, we
might reasonably wonder whether artistic and stylistic flaws
genuinely irritated some reviewers, or whether the politics
underlying the book provoked their disaffection. On the other hand,
Böll himself, as revealed in our discussion of the form of the text,
has been honest enough to admit to its limitations. It would be
inappropriate, however, to overemphasise these considerations, for
the 'Erzählung' explores, and not without telling satirical humour,
themes of crucial importance: the conflict between the individual and
the Establishment; the roles of the police, the Church, the press;
language and its implications; violence. Perhaps the highly
controversial nature of these issues caused the public to overlook the
major merits of this piece of fiction in 1974. The volatile historical
context in which the book first appeared may, but only to some
degree, justify this neglect. With the passage of time, critics will
have less and less excuse for failing to place the 'Erzählung' in
proper perspective. Future generations have a duty to ensure that this
and other works by Heinrich Böll are still read in the years to come.

REFERENCES

INTRODUCTION

1. Butler, Michael, 'The conscience of the nation', *TLS* , 15 May 1987.
2. Butler, 'Loveless, guiltless', *TLS* , 14 February 1986.
3. Hannes Kraus drew attention to the President's 'Termindilemma"in his lecture on 'Literatur und Terrorismus' at the University of Strathclyde on 20 November 1986.
4. Höllerer, Walter, 'Zum Tod von Heinrich Böll', *GQ*, 59 (1986), 103.
5. (anon.), 'Consumer Comforts', *TLS*, 1 June 1973, 604.
6. Vogt, Jochen, 'Heinrich Böll', *KLG*, September 1980, 8.
7. Reid, J. H., 'Back to the Billiards Table? - Heinrich Böll's *Fürsorgliche Belagerung*', *FMLS*, 19 (1983), 126.
8. Glees, Anthony, 'Propagandists of the deed', *TLS*, 16-22 October 1987, 1130.
9. I base my account in the following paragraphs of the events between 1967 and 1977 on a useful hand-out distributed by Hannes Kraus (see note 3).
10. Fuentes, Carlos, and Hugh Herbert, 'Interest rates are a sin against the Holy Ghost, but you can't run an economy without them . . .', *The Guardian*, 7 May 1987.
11. Details quoted in: Schröter, Klaus, *Heinrich Böll*, (Hamburg, 1982), p.107.
12. Details in: Petersen, Anette, *Die Rezeption von Bölls >Katharina Blum< in den Massenmedien der Bundesrepublik Deutschland*, (Copenhagen/Munich, 1980), pp.16-17.
13. Details in: *der literat*, ZEITSCHRIFT FÜR LITERATUR UND KUNST, July 1987, 181.

FORM

1. Haffmans, Gerd, (ed.), *Über Alfred Andersch*, (Zurich, 1980), p.221.
2. Andersch, Alfred, *Efraim*, (Zurich, 1976), p.118.
3. Quoted in: Ellis, John. M., *Narration in the German Novelle. Theory and Interpretation*, (Cambridge, 1974), p.19, note 2.
4. Ibid., pp.2-3.

5. McGowan, Moray,"'Pale Mother, Pale Daughter? Some Reflections on Böll's Leni Gruyten and Katharina Blum', *GLL*, 37 (1984), 222.
6. Quoted in: Holbeche, Yvonne, 'Carneval in Cologne: A Reading of Heinrich Böll's *Die verlorene Ehre der Katharina Blum*', *aumla* 63.
7. Winter, Hans-Gerhard, 'Von der Dokumentarliteratur zur "neuen Subjektivität": Anmerkungen zur westdeutschen Literatur der siebziger Jahre', *Seminar*, 17 (1981), 97.

THE INDIVIDUAL

1. McGowan, op. cit., 222.
2. Schröter, op. cit., p.108.

THE POLICE

1. Quoted on back cover of Böll's *Fürsorgliche Belagerung* (dtv 10001).
2. Ludwig, Gerd, *Sprache und Wirklichkeit in Heinrich Bölls DIE VERLORENE EHRE DER KATHARINA BLUM*, (Hollfeld/Ofr., 1983), p.113.

THE CHURCH

1. Macpherson, Enid, *Heinrich Böll*, (London, 1972), pp.42-43.
2. Schröter, op. cit., p.40.
3. Tomforde, Anna, 'Pope urges Germans to share wealth with needy', *The Guardian*, 4 May 1987.
4. Armstrong, George, 'Massive police guard as Waldheim sees the Pope', *The Guardian*, 26 June 1987. Glenny, Misha, 'Waldheim visit a debacle for the Vatican', *The Guardian*, 23 June 1987.
5. Macpherson, op. cit., p.41.
6. Böll, *Ansichten eines Clowns*, (dtv 400), p.1,77.

THE PRESS

1. Ludwig, op. cit., p.1.
2. McGowan, op. cit., 222.
3. Wallraff, Günter, *Der Aufmacher. Der Mann, der bei*

'Bild''Hans Esser war, (Cologne, 1977); *Zeugen der Anklage.*
Die 'Bild'-Beschreibung wird fortgesetzt, (Cologne, 1979);
Bild-Störung: Ein Handbuch, (Hamburg, 1981).

LANGUAGE

1. Andersch, *Einige Zeichnungen*, (Zurich, 1977), p.7; *öffentlicher Brief*, (Zurich, 1977), p.123, 112.
2. Andersch, *Efraim's Book*, King Penguin, p.67.
3. Schröter, op. cit., p.61.
4. Ibid., p.84.
5. Vogt, op. cit., p.12.
6. In: dell'Agli, Anna Maria, (ed.), *Zu Heinrich Böll*, (Stuttgart, 1983), p.88.
7. Ibid., p.97.

VIOLENCE

1. Haffmans, Gerd, (ed.), *Das Alfred Andersch Lesebuch*, (Zurich, 1979), p.93.
2. Schröter, op. cit., p.69.
3. Ibid., p.97.
4. Schmidt, Arno, *Der Briefwechsel mit Alfred Andersch*, (Zurich, 1985).
5. Haffmans, *Über Alfred Andersch*, (Zurich, 1980), p.209.
6. Schröter, op. cit., p.119.
7. Ibid., p.118.
8. Reid, op. cit., 134.

CONCLUSION

1. Sharpe, Lesley, 'Der Verbrecher aus verlorener Ehre : An Early Exercise in Schillerian Psychology', *GLL*, 33 (1980), 104.
2. Schiller, *Wallensteins Tod*, (Stuttgart, 1979), (Universal-Bibliothek Nr.42).
3. Schröter, op. cit., pp.35, 37.
4. Kieser, Rolf, 'An interview with Max Frisch', in: Dembo, L. S., (ed.), *Interviews with Contemporary Writers. Second Series, 1972-1982* , (Wisconsin, 1983, p.10.
5. 'Commentary', *TLS*, 27 October 1972, 1284.
6. Vogt, op. cit., p.17.

SELECT BIBLIOGRAPHY

PRIMARY LITERATURE

Böll, Heinrich, *Ende einer Dienstfahrt*, (Cologne, 1966)
--- *Die verlorene Ehre der Katharina Blum*, (Cologne, 1974). (also: Munich 1976/1985, dtv 1150; (ed.) Ulrike Hanna Meinhof and Ruth Bach, Harrap's Modern World Literature Series 1980/1986; translated by Leila Vennewitz, Secker and Warburg 1975, and Penguin Books 1978/1984)
--- *Berichte zur Gesinnungslage der Nation*, (Cologne, 1975)
--- *Fürsorgliche Belagerung*, (Cologne, 1979)
--- *Werke. Essayistische Schriften und Reden 2. 1964-1972*, (ed.) Bernd Balzer, (Cologne, 1978)
--- *Werke. Interviews I. 1961-1978*, (ed.) Bernd Balzer, (Cologne, 1978)

SECONDARY LITERATURE

Books

dell'Agli, Anna Maria, (ed.), *Zu Heinrich Böll*, (Stuttgart, 1983)
Grützbach, Franz, (ed.), *Heinrich Böll: Freies Geleit für Ulrike Meinhof. Ein Artikel und seine Folgen*, (Cologne, 1972)
Hoffmann, Gabriele, *Heinrich Böll*, (Bornheim-Merten, 1986)
[Inter Nationes], *Heinrich Böll. On His Death. Selected Obituaries and the last interview*, (Bonn, 1985)
Kilborn, R. W., *Whose Lost Honour?*, (Glasgow, 1984)
Linder, Christian, *Drei Tage im März. Ein Gespräch mit Heinrich Böll*, (Cologne, 1975)
Ludwig, Gerd, *Sprache und Wirklichkeit in Heinrich Bölls Erzählung DIE VERLORENE EHRE DER KATHARINA BLUM. Eine literarische Auseinandersetzung mit dem Sensationsjournalismus*, (Hollfeld/Ofr., 1983)
Macpherson, Enid, *Heinrich Böll*, (London, 1972)
Petersen, Anette, *Die Rezeption von Bölls >Katharina Blum< in den Massenmedien der Bundesrepublik Deutschland*, (Copenhagen/ Munich, 1980), (Text & Kontext. Sonderreihe, Band 9)
Reid, James, H., *Heinrich Böll. Withdrawal and Re-emergence*, (London, 1973)

Schröter, Klaus, *Heinrich Böll*, (Reinbek bei Hamburg, 1982)

Vogt, Jochen, *Heinrich Böll*, (Munich, 1978)

Articles

Bullivant, Keith, 'Heinrich Böll - A Tribute', *German Life and Letters*, 39 (1986), 245-251

Head, David, '"Der Autor muss respektiert werden". Schlöndorff/-Trotta's *Die verlorene Ehre der Katharina Blum* and Brecht's Critique of Film Adaptation', *German Life and Letters*, 32 (1979), 248-264

Holbeche, Yvonne, 'Carneval in Cologne: A Reading of Heinrich Böll's *Die verlorene Ehre der Katharina Blum*', *aumla* 63, May 1985, 33-42

Höllerer, Walter, 'Zum Tod von Heinrich Böll', *German Quarterly*, 59(1986), 103-105

McGowan, Moray, 'Pale Mother, Pale Daughter? Some Reflections on Böll's Leni Gruyten and Katharina Blum', *German Life and Letters*, 37 (1984), 218-228

Payne, Philip, 'Heinrich Böll versus Axel Springer: Some Observations on "Die verlorene Ehre der Katharina Blum"', *New German Studies*, 6 (1978), 45-57

Rectanus, Mark W., 'The Lost Honor of Katharina Blum:: The Reception of a German Best-Seller in the USA', *German Quarterly*, 59 (1986), 252-269

Vogt, Jochen, 'Heinrich Böll', *Kritisches Lexikon der deutschen Gegenwartsliteratur*, Stand: 1 September 1980, 1-17 and A-O

Williams, Rhys W., 'Heinrich Böll and the Katharina Blum Debate', *Critical Quarterly*, 21 (1979), 49-58